Growing in the Gospel

The Psalms Project Volume Five

Discovering the Spiritual World through the Psalms – Psalm 41-50

Michael Harvey Koplitz

TABLE OF CONTENTS

The goal of this project:

This research project will examine the 150 psalms for the spiritual awareness each Psalm offers. Each Psalm will be examined by its language and the commentary of the Sages. The spiritual awareness analysis will be done in alignment with Ari's definition of the Tree of life, the Book of Creation, and the Zohar. Each verse of the Psalm will be rewritten using the intent of the language and spiritual commentary to convey its spiritual lesson.

The main resources:

The Zohar

The Book of Creation

Ari's writing on the Tree of Life and the Ten Sefirot

The Theological Wordbook of the Old Testament

Samson Hirsch's commentary on the Psalms

Tehillim – Psalms – A new translation with a commentary anthologized from the Talmudic and rabbinic sources

Accordance Bible Software

Psalm 41

New American Standard 1995	Hebrew

Psa. 41:0 For the choir director. A Psalm of David.
 	
Psa. 41:1   How blessed is he who [a]considers the [1]helpless;
      The LORD will deliver him [b]in a day of [2]trouble.
2   The LORD will [a]protect him and keep him alive,
      And he shall [1]be called [b]blessed upon the earth;
      And [c]do not give him over to the desire of his enemies.
3   The LORD will sustain him upon his sickbed;
      In his illness, You [1]restore him to health.
 	
Psa. 41:4   As for me, I said, "O LORD, be gracious to me;
      [a]Heal my soul, for [b]I have sinned against You."
5   My enemies [a]speak evil against me,
      "When will he die, and his name perish?"
6   And [1]when he comes to see *me,* he [a]speaks [2]falsehood;
      His heart gathers wickedness to itself;
      When he goes outside, he tells it.
7   All who hate me whisper together against me;
      Against me they [a]devise my hurt, *saying,*
	לַמְנַצֵּחַ מִזְמוֹר Psa. 41:1
	לְדָוִד׃ 2 אַשְׁרֵי מַשְׂכִּיל אֶל־
	דָּל בְּיוֹם רָעָה יְמַלְּטֵהוּ
	יְהֹוָה׃ 3 יְהֹוָה ׀ יִשְׁמְרֵהוּ
	וִיחַיֵּהוּ יֻאֻשַּׁר [וּ][אֻשַּׁר]
	בָּאָרֶץ וְאַל־תִּתְּנֵהוּ בְּנֶפֶשׁ
	אֹיְבָיו׃ 4 יְהֹוָה יִסְעָדֶנּוּ עַל־
	עֶרֶשׂ דְּוָי כָּל־מִשְׁכָּבוֹ הָפַכְתָּ
	בְחָלְיוֹ׃ 5 אֲנִי־אָמַרְתִּי יְהֹוָה
	חָנֵּנִי רְפָאָה נַפְשִׁי כִּי־
	חָטָאתִי לָךְ׃ 6 אוֹיְבַי יֹאמְרוּ
	רַע לִי מָתַי יָמוּת וְאָבַד
	שְׁמוֹ׃ 7 וְאִם־בָּא לִרְאוֹת ׀
	שָׁוְא יְדַבֵּר לִבּוֹ יִקְבָּץ־אָוֶן
	לוֹ יֵצֵא לַחוּץ יְדַבֵּר׃ 8 יַחַד
	עָלַי יִתְלַחֲשׁוּ כָּל־שֹׂנְאָי עָלַי ׀
	יַחְשְׁבוּ רָעָה לִי׃ 9 דְּבַר־
	בְּלִיַּעַל יָצוּק בּוֹ וַאֲשֶׁר שָׁכַב
	לֹא־יוֹסִיף לָקוּם׃ 10 גַּם־אִישׁ

8 "A wicked thing is poured out
[1]upon him,

That when he lies down, he will
[a]not rise up again."

9 Even my [a]close friend in whom I trusted,

Who ate my bread,

Has lifted up his heel against me.

Psa. 41:10 But You, O LORD, be gracious to me and [a]raise me up,

That I may repay them.

11 By this I know that [a]You are pleased with me,

Because [b]my enemy does not shout in triumph over me.

12 As for me, [a]You uphold me in my integrity,

And You set me [b]in Your presence forever.

Psa. 41:13 [a]Blessed be the LORD, the God of Israel,

From everlasting to everlasting.
Amen and Amen.

שְׁלוֹמִ֨י ׀ אֲשֶׁר־בָּטַ֣חְתִּי ב֑וֹ
אוֹכֵ֥ל לַ֝חְמִ֗י הִגְדִּ֥יל עָלַ֥י
עָקֵֽב׃ 11 וְאַתָּ֤ה יְהוָ֗ה חָנֵּ֥נִי
וַהֲקִימֵ֑נִי וַאֲשַׁלְּמָ֥ה לָהֶֽם׃ 12
בְּזֹ֣את יָ֭דַעְתִּי כִּי־חָפַ֣צְתָּ בִּ֑י
כִּ֤י לֹֽא־יָרִ֖יעַ אֹיְבִ֣י עָלָֽי׃ 13
וַאֲנִ֗י בְּ֭תֻמִּי תָּמַ֣כְתָּ בִּ֑י
וַתַּצִּיבֵ֖נִי לְפָנֶ֣יךָ לְעוֹלָֽם׃ 14
בָּר֤וּךְ יְהוָ֨ה ׀ אֱלֹהֵ֪י יִשְׂרָאֵ֡ל
מֵֽהָע֬וֹלָם וְעַ֤ד הָעוֹלָ֗ם אָ֘מֵ֥ן ׀
וְאָמֵֽן׃

References

Psalm 41:1
[1]Or *poor*
[2]Or *evil*
[a]Ps 82:3, 4; Prov 14:21
[b]Ps 27:5; 37:19

Psalm 41:2
[1]Or *be blessed*
[a]Ps 37:28
[b]Ps 37:22
[c]Ps 27:12

Psalm 41:3
[1]Lit *turn all his bed*

Psalm 41:4
[a]Ps 6:2; 103:3; 147:3
[b]Ps 51:4

Psalm 41:5
[a]Ps 38:12

Psalm 41:6
[1]Or *if he*
[2]Or *emptiness*
[a]Ps 12:2; 62:4; Prov 26:24-26

Psalm 41:7
[a]Ps 56:5

Psalm 41:8
[1]Or *within*
[a]Ps 71:10, 11

Psalm 41:9
[a]2 Sam 15:12; Job 19:13, 19; Ps 55:12, 13, 20; Jer 20:10; Mic 7:5; Matt 26:23; Luke 22:21; John 13:18

Psalm 41:10
[a]Ps 3:3

Psalm 41:11
[a]Ps 37:23; 147:11
[b]Ps 25:2

Psalm 41:12
[a]Ps 18:32; 37:17; 63:8
[b]Job 36:7; Ps 21:6

Psalm 41:13
[a]Ps 72:18, 19; 89:52; 106:48; 150:6

Targum

Psa. 41:1 For praise; a psalm of David. ² Happy the man who is wise to show mercy to the humble and poor on the day of evil; the LORD will deliver him. ³ The LORD will keep him and preserve him and do well to him in the land; and he will not hand him over to the will of his enemies. ⁴ The word of the LORD will aid him in his life, and be revealed to him on the bed of his sickness to preserve him; you have reversed wholly his bed in the time of his sickness and rebuke. ⁵ I said: O LORD, have mercy on me; heal my soul, for I have sinned in your presence. ⁶ My enemies will speak evil about me: "When will he die and his name perish?" ⁷ And if he comes to welcome me, he will speak falsehood; in his mind he will gather iniquity to himself, he will go outside [and] speak. ⁸ All my enemies speak together about me in secret, plotting ruin for me. ⁹ He will pour out on him the speech of an oppressor, and will say, "This one who is sick will not get up again." ¹⁰ Even a man who seeks my welfare, in whom I trusted, feeding him my meal – he has cunningly prevailed over me. ¹¹ But you, O LORD, have mercy on me, and raise me up from illness; and I will pay them back. ¹² By this I know that you have favored me, that my enemy has not prevailed over me to cause harm. ¹³ But I, for my blamelessness – you have sustained me; and you made me stand in your presence forever. ¹⁴ Blessed be the name of the LORD God of Israel, from this world to the world to come; the righteous will say, "Amen and amen."

Spiritual Awareness

The spiritual rewrite for the verses is in bold.

Introduction

In David's day, sickness was considered a push from the LORD because He was displeased with something in one's morality. David was upset because he had an illness that prevented him from building the LORD's Temple in Jerusalem. However, the LORD cured him of his illness so that he could gather together the materials and develop the plans for the Temple that his son Solomo was going to complete.

Superscript

לַמְנַצֵּחַ מִזְמוֹר לְדָוִד (lam'nctzacha meez'mor l'david) – means "To Him who grants victory, a psalm of David." The spiritual awareness in this superscript is that David called upon the Sefirah Netzach for success over his illness and enemies.

To Netzach, a Psalm of David.

Verse one, two, and three

There is a constant shift between the second and third person, making it difficult to interpret the verses. Spiritual awareness is found in Hirsch's translation.

Progress is with him who gives understanding care to him that has been brought low; the LORD will deliver him on the day of disaster.

The LORD will preserve him and keep him alive, and he will yet be happy on earth; but, even so, you shall not deliver him up to the will of his foes.

The LORD will not let him grow strong upon his bed of illness, but it is you who shall then have transfigured all his lying down during his sickness.

Verses four to nine

David experienced something different during his illness. He prayed for help for the healing of his soul. His enemies rejoiced when they saw his affliction. They wanted him to die. Nevertheless, the LORD did not let David die. He was healed to confront his enemies and be victorious through the Sefirah Netzach.

As for me, I have said, "O LORD grant me Your favor; heal my soul, for I have sinned against You.

My enemies, however, speak evil of me: "When will he die, and his name disappear?"

And if one comes to visit, he speaks only falsehood; his heart gathers that which is used for evil so that once he has gone out, he can speak of it.

They that hate me whisper together against me; they sit beside me and devise evil for me.

An incurable ill has been cast upon him; now that he is laid low he shall rise again no more.

Even the man of my peace in whom I had put my trust, who eats my bread, lifts up his heel against me in contempt.

Verses 10 and 11

But You, O LORD, deal kindly with me and raise me up, and then I shall repay them.

By this I know that You are pleased with me, because my enemy does not shout in triumph over me.

Verse 12

David was aware that the LORD's support would always be with him as long as he devoted himself to the discharge of his tasks and duties

As for me, You uphold me in my integrity, and You set me in Your presence forever.

Verse 13

בָּרוּךְ **(Baruch)** – means "blessed." In this verse, it means "furthered and brought ever closer to full realization."

Blessed be the LORD, the God of Israel, from everlasting to everlasting. Amen and Amen.

Complete Psalm Rewrite Emphasizing Spiritual Awareness

To Netzach, a Psalm of David.

Progress is with him who gives understanding care to him that has been brought low; the LORD will deliver him on the day of disaster.

The LORD will preserve him and keep him alive and he will yet be happy on earth; but, even so, you shall not deliver him up to the will of his foes.

The LORD will not let him grow strong upon his bed of illness, but it is you who shall then have transfigured all his lying down during his sickness.

As for me, I have said, "O LORD grant me Your favor; heal my soul, for I have sinned against You.

My enemies, however, speak evil of me: "When will he die, and his name disappear?"

And if one comes to visit, he speaks only falsehood; his heart gathers that which is used for evil so that once he has gone out, he can speak of it.

They that hate me whisper together against me; they sit beside me and devise evil for me.

An incurable ill has been cast upon him; now that he is laid low he shall rise again no more.

Even the man of my peace in whom I had put my trust, who eats my bread, lifts up his heel against me in contempt.

But You, O LORD, deal kindly with me and raise me up, and then I shall repay them. By this I know that You are pleased with me, because my enemy does not shout in triumph over me.

As for me, You uphold me in my integrity, and You set me in Your presence forever.

Blessed be the LORD, the God of Israel, from everlasting to everlasting. Amen and Amen.

Psalm 42

New American Standard 1995	Hebrew

Psa. 42:0 For the choir director. A †Maskil of the sons of Korah.

Psa. 42:1 As the deer [1]pants for the water brooks,
> So my soul [1a]pants for You, O God.
[2] My soul [a]thirsts for God, for the [b]living God;
> When shall I come and [1c]appear before God?
[3] My [a]tears have been my food day and night,
> While *they* [b]say to me all day long, "Where is your God?"
[4] These things I remember and I [a]pour out my soul within me.
> For I [b]used to go along with the throng *and* [1]lead them in procession to the house of God,
> With the voice of [j]joy and thanksgiving, a multitude keeping festival.

Psa. 42:5 [a]Why are you [1b]in despair, O my soul?
> And *why* have you become [c]disturbed within me?
> [2d]Hope in God, for I shall [3]again praise [4]Him
> *For* the [5e]help of His presence.
[6] O my God, my soul is [1]in despair within me;
> Therefore I [a]remember You from [b]the land of the Jordan

לְמְנַצֵּחַ מַשְׂכִּיל Psa. 42:1
לִבְנֵי־קֹרַח ׃ 2 כְּאַיָּל תַּעֲרֹג
עַל־אֲפִיקֵי־מָיִם כֵּן נַפְשִׁי
תַעֲרֹג אֵלֶיךָ אֱלֹהִים ׃ 3
צָמְאָה נַפְשִׁי ׀ לֵאלֹהִים לְאֵל
חָי מָתַי אָבוֹא וְאֵרָאֶה פְּנֵי
אֱלֹהִים ׃ 4 הָיְתָה־לִּי דִמְעָתִי
לֶחֶם יוֹמָם וָלַיְלָה בֶּאֱמֹר
אֵלַי כָּל־הַיּוֹם אַיֵּה אֱלֹהֶיךָ ׃
5 אֵלֶּה אֶזְכְּרָה ׀ וְאֶשְׁפְּכָה
עָלַי ׀ נַפְשִׁי כִּי אֶעֱבֹר ׀ בַּסָּךְ
אֶדַּדֵּם עַד־בֵּית אֱלֹהִים
בְּקוֹל־רִנָּה וְתוֹדָה הָמוֹן
חוֹגֵג ׃ 6 מַה־תִּשְׁתּוֹחֲחִי ׀
נַפְשִׁי וַתֶּהֱמִי עָלָי הוֹחִילִי
לֵאלֹהִים כִּי־עוֹד אוֹדֶנּוּ
יְשׁוּעוֹת פָּנָיו ׃ 7 אֱלֹהַי עָלַי
נַפְשִׁי תִשְׁתּוֹחָח עַל־כֵּן
אֶזְכָּרְךָ מֵאֶרֶץ יַרְדֵּן
וְחֶרְמוֹנִים מֵהַר מִצְעָר ׃ 8

And the [2]peaks of [c]Hermon, from Mount Mizar.

7 Deep calls to deep at the sound of Your waterfalls;

All Your [a]breakers and Your waves have rolled over me.

8 The LORD will [a]command His lovingkindness in the daytime;

And His song will be with me [b]in the night,

A prayer to [c]the God of my life.

Psa. 42:9 I will say to God [a]my rock, "Why have You forgotten me?

Why do I go [b]mourning [1]because of the [c]oppression of the enemy?"

10 As a shattering of my bones, my adversaries revile me,

While they [a]say to me all day long, "Where is your God?"

11 [a]Why are you [1]in despair, O my soul?

And why have you become disturbed within me?

[2]Hope in God, for I shall yet praise Him,

The [3]help of my countenance and my God.

תְּהוֹם־אֶל־תְּהוֹם קוֹרֵא לְקוֹל צִנּוֹרֶיךָ כָּל־מִשְׁבָּרֶיךָ וְגַלֶּיךָ עָלַי עָבָרוּ | 9 יוֹמָם | יְצַוֶּה יְהוָה | חַסְדּוֹ וּבַלַּיְלָה שִׁירֹה [שִׁירוֹ] עִמִּי תְּפִלָּה לְאֵל חַיָּי : 10 אוֹמְרָה | לְאֵל סַלְעִי לָמָה שְׁכַחְתָּנִי לָמָה־קֹדֵר אֵלֵךְ בְּלַחַץ אוֹיֵב : 11 בְּרֶצַח | בְּעַצְמוֹתַי חֵרְפוּנִי צוֹרְרָי בְּאָמְרָם אֵלַי כָּל־הַיּוֹם אַיֵּה אֱלֹהֶיךָ : 12 מַה־תִּשְׁתּוֹחֲחִי | וַנַפְשִׁי וּמַה־תֶּהֱמִי עָלָי הוֹחִילִי לֵאלֹהִים כִּי־עוֹד אוֹדֶנּוּ יְשׁוּעֹת פָּנַי וֵאלֹהָי :

References

<table>
<tr><td valign="top" width="50%">

Psalm 42:1
[1]Lit *longs for*
[a]Ps 119:131

Psalm 42:2
[1]Some mss read *see the face of God*
[a]Ps 63:1; 84:2; 143:6
[b]Josh 3:10; Ps 84:2; Jer 10:10; Dan 6:26; Matt 26:63; Rom 9:26; 1 Thess 1:9
[c]Ex 23:17; Ps 43:4; 84:7

Psalm 42:3
[a]Ps 80:5; 102:9
[b]Ps 79:10; 115:2; Joel 2:17; Mic 7:10

Psalm 42:4
[1]Or *move slowly with them*
[a]1 Sam 1:15; Job 30:16; Ps 62:8; Lam 2:19
[b]Ps 55:14; 122:1; Is 30:29
[c]Ps 100:4

Psalm 42:5
[1]Or *sunk down*
[2]Or *Wait for*
[3]Or *still*
[4]Some ancient versions read *Him, the help of my countenance and my God*
[5]Or *saving acts of*
[a]Ps 42:11; 43:5
[b]Ps 38:6; Matt 26:38
[c]Ps 77:3
[d]Ps 71:14; Lam 3:24
[e]Ps 44:3

</td><td valign="top" width="50%">

Psalm 42:6
[1]Or *sunk down*
[2]Lit *Hermons*
[a]Ps 61:2
[b]2 Sam 17:22
[c]Deut 3:8

Psalm 42:7
[a]Ps 69:1, 2; 88:7; Jon 2:3

Psalm 42:8
[a]Ps 57:3; 133:3
[b]Job 35:10; Ps 16:7; 63:6; 77:6; 149:5
[c]Eccl 5:18; 8:15

Psalm 42:9
[1]Or *while the enemy oppresses*
[a]Ps 18:2
[b]Ps 38:6
[c]Ps 17:9

Psalm 42:10
[a]Ps 42:3; Joel 2:17

Psalm 42:11
[1]Or *sunk down*
[2]Or *Wait for*
[3]Or *saving acts of*
[a]Ps 42:5; 43:5

</td></tr>
</table>

Targum

Psa. 42:1 For praise, with good discernment, by the sons of Korah. **2** As the deer that longs for streams of water, thus my soul longs for you, O LORD. **3** My soul is thirsty for you, for the mighty, living, and enduring God. When will I enter and see the splendor of the presence of the LORD? **4** My tears have become my sustenance day and night, because the enemy says to me all day, "Where is your God?" **5** These miracles I remember; and I will pour out the thoughts of my soul whenever I pass beneath the shelter alone; I will be strong in the camps of the righteous, [who are going] to the sanctuary of the LORD with a voice of petition and praise, a tumult of peoples coming to keep festival in Jerusalem. **6** Why will you be lowly, O my soul, and [why] will you rage against me? Wait for God, for again I will praise him for the redemption that is from his presence. **7** O God, my soul will be for me lowly, therefore I will remember you [among] those who dwell yonder in the land of Jordan, and those who dwell on the mountains of Hermoni, and the people who accepted the Torah on mount Sinai, which is lowly and small. **8** The upper deep calls to the lower deep, at the sound of the pouring of spouts – thus all your breakers and waves passed over me at the time we came forth from Egypt. **9** By day the LORD will command his goodness, and by night his praise is with me, a prayer to the God who preserves my life. **10** I will say to God my trust, "Why have you neglected me, why do I go about in darkness in the oppression of the enemy?" **11** Because they kill my bones whenever my oppressors mock me, when they say to me every day, "Where is your God?" **12** Why will you be lowly, O my soul, and [why] will you rage against me? Wait for God, for again I will praise him for the redemption that comes from his presence, for he is my God.

Spiritual Awareness

The spiritual rewrite for the verses are in bold.

Introduction

This psalms is the beginning of the second book of Psalms. The first forty-one psalms were attributed to David. The sons of Korach wrote the next eight hymns. Rashi said that the sons of Korach initially joined their father's infamous rebellion against Moses and Aaron. During the rebellion, the three sons realized the folly of their error and repented for their involvement. The Earth opened up and swallowed the entire assembly of Korach and sent them to Gehinnom. The LORD miraculously provided a place of refuge for Korach's three sons.

When they ascended to the Earth's surface, a Spirit of the LORD descended upon them. They prophesied the Exile of Israel, the destruction of the Temple in Jerusalem, and the advent of the Davidic monarchy. This psalm is the Song of the Day for the second day of the Sukkot festival. The Festival of the Water Drawing began on this day in the Temple.

The Festival of the Water Drawing Day - "At this most joyous season of the year, with all the electric anticipation along the caravan trails, the stirring ceremonies, and the lively singing and feasting, the epitome of celebration in Temple times took place surrounding a water ritual: the Rejoicing *(Simchat)* at the Place of *(Beit)* the Water Drawing *(Hashoavah)*.

Every day of the year, after the sacrifice was burned, an offering of wine was poured on the altar. During Sukkot, there was also a water libation *(nisukh hamayim)*. Some have suggested that it was a folk rite, an inducement for rain made by pouring out water at the season's onset, transformed by the rabbis into a symbolic Temple ritual.

Each morning of Sukkot, the priests went to the pool of Siloah (Silwan) near Jerusalem to fill a golden flask. Shofar blasts greeted their arrival at the Temple's Water Gate. They then ascended and poured the water so that it flowed over the altar simultaneously with wine from another bowl. When the priest was about to pour the water, the people shouted "Raise your hand!" because of an incident that occurred in a previous year: The high priest Alexander Jannaeus (103-76 B.C.E.) showed contempt for the rite by spilling the water at his feet, a transgression for which worshippers threw their citrons at him."[1]

Superscript

לַמְנַצֵּחַ (lam'natzecha) – means "to who grants victory." This psalm is an appeal to the Sefirah Netzach, who offers victory. The NASB does not translate this word properly. It uses the translation "for the choir director," which is not correct.

To Him who grants victory, an instruction by the sons of Korach.

---

[1] Lesli Koppelman Ross, "Simchat Beit Hashoavah: The Water-Drawing Festival," My Jewish Learning, October 16, 2017, https://www.myjewishlearning.com/article/simchat-beit-hashoavah-the-water-drawing-festival/.

Verse One

כְּאַיָּל תַּעֲרֹג (keearal taarog) – means "as the deer pants." Hirsch argues that this phrase should be read as "as the deer cries." The roe deer makes a peculiar cry. The understanding of crying comes from Joel 1:20 because of the usage of the words. Since the psalm is a cry for help, this understanding of the phrase applies to this psalm.

As the roe deer cries for the springs of water above, so my soul thirsts after You, O God.

Verse two

The psalmist distinguishes between the living God of Israel and against the "dead" idols of the nations that surround Israel.

My soul thirsts for God, for the living God and not the dead idols of the nations that surround us; when shall I come and envision myself before the countenance of God?

Verse three

Israel yeared for the LORD. It is so great that it did not feel the desire for any other kind of nourishment. Its spiritual needs were satisfied. The nation knew that it stood alone and surrounded by idol worshipers. Israel knew that she belonged to the LORD.

My tears have been my bread day and night, while the surrounding nations say, "Where is your God?"

Verse four

The nation remembers the climax of its past glory, the pilgrimage festivals, when the entire nation, gathering from all parts, wandered up to its focal point at the Temple in Jerusalem. This rallied and unified the nation.

These things I remember, and I pour out my soul within me, for I used to go along with the throng and lead them in procession to the house of God, with the voice of joy and thanksgiving, a multitude keeping festival.

Verse five

The nation needed to have courage. This verse says that hope in God is necessary for the good life.

Why are you in despair, O my soul? And *why* have you become disturbed within me? Hope in God, for I shall again praise Him *for* the help of His presence.

Verse six

Thanksgiving is offered for the Promised Land.

O my God, my soul is in despair within me; Therefore I remember You from the land of the Jordan and the peaks of Hermon, from Mount Mizar.

Verse Seven

The allegory of "floods of water" has been used in Scripture to denote pain or suffering.

Now, too, deep calls unto deep to obey your guidance; they are all Your billows and Your waves that have gone over me.

Verse Eight

The Sefirah Chesed will always shower Israel with the LORD's loving and kindness.

By the light of day, the LORD will have the Sefirah Chesed send his loving kindness, and even in the night, His song, the song of the God, is with me, a prayer for the God of my life.

Verse nine

There are times that the people of Israel thought that the LORD had forgotten them.

I say to God, my Rock, "Why would You have forgotten me? Why should I go mourning under the oppression of the foe?"

Verse Ten

The enemies of Israel were breaking their bones. The nation was helpless against its enemies.

While putting murder into my bones, my oppressors revile me, saying to me all the day, "Where is your God?"

Verse eleven

Israel discovered that there has never been a conflict between the goals set by the LORD and those toward which the nation must strive in truth. Israel will come to realize that even in the dark times, they served the LORD to advance genuine truth, happiness and fulfill the destiny that is the goal of its mission in the history of the world.

Why are you in despair, O my soul? And why have you become disturbed within me? Hope in God, for I shall yet praise Him, the help of my countenance and my God.

Complete Psalm Rewrite Emphasizing Spiritual Awareness

As the roe deer cries for the springs of water above, so my soul thirsts after You, O God.

My soul thirsts for God, for the living God and not the dead idols of the nations that surround us; when shall I come and envision myself before the countenance of God

My tears have been my bread day and night, while the surrounding nations say, "Where is your God?"

These things I remember, and I pour out my soul within me, for I used to go along with the throng and lead them in procession to the house of God, with the voice of joy and thanksgiving, a multitude keeping festival.

Why are you in despair, O my soul? And *why* have you become disturbed within me? Hope in God, for I shall again praise Him *for* the help of His presence.

O my God, my soul is in despair within me; Therefore I remember You from the land of the Jordan and the peaks of Hermon, from Mount Mizar.

Now, too, deep calls unto deep to obey your guidance; they are all Your billows and Your waves that have gone over me.

By the light of day, the LORD will have the Sefirah Chesed send his loving kindness, and even in the night, His song, the song of the God, is with me, a prayer for the God of my life.

I say to God, my Rock, "Why would You have forgotten me? Why should I go mourning under the oppression of the foe?"

While putting murder into my bones, my oppressors revile me, saying to me all the day, "Where is your God?"

Why are you in despair, O my soul? And why have you become disturbed within me? Hope in God, for I shall yet praise Him, the help of my countenance and my God.

Psalm 43

New American Standard 1995	Hebrew

Psa. 43:1 *a*Vindicate me, O God, and *b*plead my case against an ungodly nation;
[1]O deliver me from *c*the deceitful and unjust man!
[2]   For You are the *a*God of my strength; why have You *b*rejected me?
Why do I go *c*mourning [1]because of the oppression of the enemy?

Psa. 43:3   O send out Your *a*light and Your truth, let them lead me;
Let them bring me to Your *b*holy hill
And to Your *c*dwelling places.
[4]   Then I will go to *a*the altar of God,
To God [1]my exceeding *b*joy;
And upon the [1]lyre I shall praise You, O God, my God.

Psa. 43:5   *a*Why are you [1]in despair, O my soul?
And why are you disturbed within me?
[2]Hope in God, for I shall [3]again praise Him,
The [4]help of my countenance and my God.

References

<table>
<tr><td valign="top">

Psalm 43:1
[1]Or *May You*
[a]Ps 26:1; 35:24
[b]1 Sam 24:15; Ps 35:1
[c]Ps 5:6; 38:12

Psalm 43:2
[1]Or *while the enemy oppresses*
[a]Ps 18:1; 28:7; 31:4
[b]Ps 44:9; 88:14
[c]Ps 42:9

Psalm 43:3
[a]Ps 36:9
[b]Ps 2:6; 3:4; 42:4; 46:4
[c]Ps 84:1

Psalm 43:4
[1]Lit *the gladness of my joy*
[a]Ps 26:6
[b]Ps 21:6
[c]Ps 33:2; 49:4; 57:8; 71:22

Psalm 43:5
[1]Or *sunk down*
[2]Or *Wait for*
[3]Or *still*
[4]Or *saving acts of*
[a]Ps 42:5, 11

</td><td></td></tr>
</table>

Targum

Psa. 43:1 Judge me, O LORD with true judgment; it is for you to argue my case with a people that is not righteous; from the deceitful and oppressive man you will save me. **2** For you are God, my strength; why have you abandoned me? why do I go about in gloom at the oppression of the enemy? **3** Send your light and your faithfulness; they will guide me, they will bring me to the mount of the sanctuary and the academies, the place of your presence. **4** And I will come to make his sacrifice at the altar of my God the LORD; to my God from whom is the joy of my gladness; and I will give thanks in your presence with the lyre, O LORD my God. **5** Why will you be lowly, O my soul, and [why] will you rage against me? Wait for God, for again I will praise him for the redemption that comes from his presence, for he is my God.

Spiritual Awareness

The spiritual rewrite for the verses is in bold.

Introduction

The Sage Radak believed that this Psalm is a continuation of the preceding Psalm. In it, the author expresses a deep yearning for redemption from the agony of exile.

Verse one

מִגּוֹי לֹא־חָסִיד (meegoy lo-chaseed) – means "from ungodly people." This phrase also implies a people who fail to practice fundamental human rights. They say they do, but it is only lip service.

Judge me, O God and please my cause against a nation which does not work loving-kindness; O deliver me from a man of deceit and violence.

Verse two

The Psalmist asks the LORD why he was always given spiritual support, and now it has stopped.

You are my LORD who supplies me with spiritual support and strength; why have you taken it away? Why do I go mourning because of the oppression of the enemy?

Verse three

שְׁלַח־אוֹרְךָ וַאֲמִתְּךָ (sh'lach or'cha vaameet'cha) – means "send out Your light and truth." This phrase can be understood differently; "O grant me the enlightenment to understand the truth you have set down for me in Your Torah."

O grant me the enlightenment to understand the truth you have set down for me in Your Torah. They will bring me home to the mountain of Your Sanctuary and to Your dwelling places.

Verse four

The Psalmist tells the LORD what he will do if granted the enlightenment from verse three.

Then I will go to the altar of God, to God my exceeding joy; and upon the lyre, I shall praise You, O God, my God.

Verse five

Israel discovered that there has never been a conflict between the goals set by the LORD and those toward which the nation must strive in truth. Israel will realize that even in the dark times, they served the LORD to advance genuine truth, happiness and fulfill the destiny that is the goal of its mission in the history of the world. This is the same final verse as in Psalm 42.

Why are you in despair, O my soul? And why have you become disturbed within me? Hope in God, for I shall yet praise Him, the help of my countenance and my God.

Complete Psalm Rewrite Emphasizing Spiritual Awareness

Judge me, O God and please my cause against a nation which does not work loving-kindness; O deliver me from a man of deceit and violence.

You are my LORD who supplies me with spiritual support and strength; why have you taken it away? Why do I go mourning because of the oppression of the enemy?

O grant me the enlightenment to understand the truth you have set down for me in Your Torah. They will bring me home to the mountain of Your Sanctuary and to Your dwelling places.

Then I will go to the altar of God, to God my exceeding joy; and upon the lyre, I shall praise You, O God, my God.

Why are you in despair, O my soul? And why have you become disturbed within me?

Hope in God, for I shall yet praise Him, the help of my countenance and my God.

Psalm 44

New American Standard 1995	Hebrew
Psa. 44:0　For the choir director. A †Maskil of the sons of Korah. **Psa. 44:1**　O God, we have heard with our ears, 　　Our [a]fathers have told us 　　The [b]work that You did in their days, 　　In the [c]days of old. 2　　You with Your own hand [a]drove out the nations; 　　Then You [b]planted them; 　　You [c]afflicted the peoples, 　　Then You [d]spread them abroad. 3　　For by their own sword they [a]did not possess the land, 　　And their own arm did not save them, 　　But Your right hand and Your [b]arm and the [c]light of Your presence, 　　For You [d]favored them. **Psa. 44:4**　You are [a]my King, O God; 　　[b]Command [1]victories for Jacob. 5　　Through You we will [a]push back our adversaries; 　　Through Your name we will [b]trample down those who rise up against us. 6　　For I will [a]not trust in my bow, 　　Nor will my sword save me. 7　　But You [a]have saved us from our adversaries, 　　And You have [b]put to shame those who hate us. 8　　In God we have [a]boasted all day long,	לַמְנַצֵּחַ לִבְנֵי־קֹרַח מַשְׂכִּיל׃ ² אֱלֹהִים ׀ בְּאָזְנֵינוּ שָׁמַעְנוּ אֲבוֹתֵינוּ סִפְּרוּ־לָנוּ פֹּעַל פָּעַלְתָּ בִימֵיהֶם בִּימֵי קֶדֶם׃ ³ אַתָּה ׀ יָדְךָ גוֹיִם הוֹרַשְׁתָּ וַתִּטָּעֵם תָּרַע לְאֻמִּים וַתְּשַׁלְּחֵם׃ ⁴ כִּי לֹא בְחַרְבָּם יָרְשׁוּ אָרֶץ וּזְרוֹעָם לֹא־ הוֹשִׁיעָה לָּמוֹ כִּי־יְמִינְךָ וּזְרוֹעֲךָ וְאוֹר פָּנֶיךָ כִּי רְצִיתָם׃ ⁵ אַתָּה־הוּא מַלְכִּי אֱלֹהִים צַוֵּה יְשׁוּעוֹת יַעֲקֹב׃ ⁶ בְּךָ צָרֵינוּ נְנַגֵּחַ בְּשִׁמְךָ נָבוּס קָמֵינוּ׃ ⁷ כִּי לֹא בְקַשְׁתִּי אֶבְטָח וְחַרְבִּי לֹא תוֹשִׁיעֵנִי׃ ⁸ כִּי הוֹשַׁעְתָּנוּ מִצָּרֵינוּ וּמְשַׂנְאֵינוּ הֱבִישׁוֹתָ׃ ⁹ בֵּאלֹהִים הִלַּלְנוּ כָל־הַיּוֹם וְשִׁמְךָ ׀ לְעוֹלָם נוֹדֶה סֶלָה׃

And we will [b]give thanks to Your name forever.   [1]Selah.

Psa. 44:9   Yet You [a]have rejected *us* and brought us to [b]dishonor,

And [c]do not go out with our armies.

[10]   You cause us to [a]turn back from the adversary;

And those who hate us [b]have taken spoil for themselves.

[11]   You give us as [a]sheep [1]to be eaten

And have [b]scattered us among the nations.

[12]   You [a]sell Your people [1]cheaply,

And have not [2]profited by their sale.

[13]   You make us a [a]reproach to our neighbors,

A scoffing and a [b]derision to those around us.

[14]   You make us [a]a byword among the nations,

A [1b]laughingstock among the peoples.

[15]   All day long my dishonor is before me

And [1]my [a]humiliation has overwhelmed me,

[16]   Because of the voice of him who [a]reproaches and reviles,

Because of the presence of the [b]enemy and the avenger.

Psa. 44:17   All this has come upon us, but we have [a]not forgotten You,

And we have not [b]dealt falsely with Your covenant.

[18]   Our heart has not [a]turned back,

And our steps [b]have not deviated from Your way,

אַף־זָנַחְתָּ וַתַּכְלִימֵנוּ וְלֹא־ [10]

תֵצֵא בְּצִבְאוֹתֵינוּ : תְּשִׁיבֵנוּ [11]

אָחוֹר מִנִּי־צָר וּמְשַׂנְאֵינוּ

שָׁסוּ לָמוֹ : תִּתְּנֵנוּ כְּצֹאן [12]

מַאֲכָל וּבַגּוֹיִם זֵרִיתָנוּ : [13]

תִּמְכֹּר־עַמְּךָ בְלֹא־הוֹן וְלֹא־

רִבִּיתָ בִּמְחִירֵיהֶם : [14]

תְּשִׂימֵנוּ חֶרְפָּה לִשְׁכֵנֵינוּ לַעַג

וָקֶלֶס לִסְבִיבוֹתֵינוּ : [15]

תְּשִׂימֵנוּ מָשָׁל בַּגּוֹיִם מְנוֹד־

רֹאשׁ בַּל־אֻמִּים : כָּל־ [16]

הַיּוֹם כְּלִמָּתִי נֶגְדִּי וּבֹשֶׁת פָּנַי

כִּסָּתְנִי : מִקּוֹל מְחָרֵף [17]

וּמְגַדֵּף מִפְּנֵי אוֹיֵב וּמִתְנַקֵּם :

כָּל־זֹאת בָּאַתְנוּ וְלֹא [18]

שְׁכַחֲנוּךָ וְלֹא־שִׁקַּרְנוּ

בִּבְרִיתֶךָ : לֹא־נָסוֹג אָחוֹר [19]

לִבֵּנוּ וַתֵּט אֲשֻׁרֵינוּ מִנִּי

אָרְחֶךָ : כִּי דִכִּיתָנוּ [20]

בִּמְקוֹם תַּנִּים וַתְּכַס עָלֵינוּ

בְצַלְמָוֶת : אִם־שָׁכַחְנוּ שֵׁם [21]

<table>
<tr><td valign="top" width="50%">

19   Yet You have ^acrushed us in a place of ^bjackals

And covered us with ^cthe shadow of death.

Psa. 44:20   If we had ^aforgotten the name of our God

Or extended our ¹hands to ^ba strange god,

21   Would not God ^afind this out?

For He knows the secrets of the heart.

22   But ^afor Your sake we are killed all day long;

We are considered as ^bsheep to be slaughtered.

23   ^aArouse Yourself, why ^bdo You sleep, O Lord?

Awake, ^cdo not reject us forever.

24   Why do You ^ahide Your face

And ^bforget our affliction and our oppression?

25   For our ^asoul has sunk down into the dust;

Our body cleaves to the earth.

26   ^aRise up, be our help,

And ^bredeem us for the sake of Your lovingkindness.

</td><td valign="top" width="50%" dir="rtl">

אֱלֹהֵינוּ וַנִּפְרֹשׂ כַּפֵּינוּ לְאֵל

זָר: 22 הֲלֹא אֱלֹהִים יַחֲקָר־

זֹאת כִּי־הוּא יֹדֵעַ תַּעֲלֻמוֹת

לֵב: 23 כִּי־עָלֶיךָ הֹרַגְנוּ

כָל־הַיּוֹם נֶחְשַׁבְנוּ כְּצֹאן

טִבְחָה: 24 עוּרָה לָמָּה

תִישַׁן אֲדֹנָי הָקִיצָה אַל־

תִּזְנַח לָנֶצַח: 25 לָמָּה־פָנֶיךָ

תַסְתִּיר תִּשְׁכַּח עָנְיֵנוּ

וְלַחֲצֵנוּ: 26 כִּי שָׁחָה לֶעָפָר

נַפְשֵׁנוּ דָּבְקָה לָאָרֶץ בִּטְנֵנוּ:

27 קוּמָה עֶזְרָתָה לָּנוּ וּפְדֵנוּ

לְמַעַן חַסְדֶּךָ:

</td></tr>
</table>

References

<table>
<tr><td>

Psalm 44:1
[a]Ex 12:26, 27; Deut 6:20; Judg 6:13; Ps 78:3
[b]Ps 78:12
[c]Deut 32:7; Ps 77:5; Is 51:9; 63:9

Psalm 44:2
[a]Josh 3:10; Neh 9:24; Ps 78:55; 80:8
[b]Ex 15:17; 2 Sam 7:10; Jer 24:6; Amos 9:15
[c]Ps 135:10-12
[d]Ps 80:9-11; Zech 2:6

Psalm 44:3
[a]Deut 8:17, 18; Josh 24:12
[b]Ps 77:15
[c]Ps 4:6; 89:15
[d]Deut 4:37; 7:7, 8; 10:15; Ps 106:4

Psalm 44:4
[1]Lit *salvation*
[a]Ps 74:12
[b]Ps 42:8

Psalm 44:5
[a]Deut 33:17; Ps 60:12; Dan 8:4
[b]Ps 108:13; Zech 10:5

Psalm 44:6
[a]1 Sam 17:47; Ps 33:16; Hos 1:7

Psalm 44:7
[a]Ps 136:24
[b]Ps 53:5

Psalm 44:8
[1]*Selah* may mean: *Pause, Crescendo* or *Musical interlude*
[a]Ps 34:2
[b]Ps 30:12

</td><td>

Psalm 44:9
[a]Ps 43:2; 60:1, 10; 74:1; 89:38; 108:11
[b]Ps 69:19
[c]Ps 60:10; 108:11

Psalm 44:10
[a]Lev 26:17; Josh 7:8, 12; Ps 89:43
[b]Ps 89:41

Psalm 44:11
[1]Lit *for food*
[a]Ps 44:22; Rom 8:36
[b]Lev 26:33; Deut 4:27; 28:64; Ps 106:27; Ezek 20:23

Psalm 44:12
[1]Lit *for no wealth*
[2]Or *set a high price on them*
[a]Deut 32:30; Judg 2:14; 3:8; Is 52:3, 4; Jer 15:13

Psalm 44:13
[a]Deut 28:37; Ps 79:4; 89:41
[b]Ps 80:6; Ezek 23:32

Psalm 44:14
[1]Lit *shaking of the head*
[a]Job 17:6; Ps 69:11; Jer 24:9
[b]2 Kin 19:21; Ps 109:25

Psalm 44:15
[1]Lit *the shame of my face has covered me*
[a]2 Chr 32:21; Ps 69:7

Psalm 44:16
[a]Ps 74:10
[b]Ps 8:2

</td></tr>
</table>

Psalm 44:17
[a]Ps 78:7; 119:61, 83, 109, 141, 153, 176
[b]Ps 78:57

Psalm 44:18
[a]Ps 78:57
[b]Job 23:11; Ps 119:51, 157

Psalm 44:19
[a]Ps 51:8; 94:5
[b]Job 30:29; Is 13:22; Jer 9:11
[c]Job 3:5; Ps 23:4

Psalm 44:20
[1]Lit *palms*
[a]Ps 78:11
[b]Deut 6:14; Ps 81:9

Psalm 44:21
[a]Ps 139:1, 2; Jer 17:10

Psalm 44:22
[a]Rom 8:36
[b]Is 53:7; Jer 12:3

Psalm 44:23
[a]Ps 7:6
[b]Ps 78:65
[c]Ps 77:7

Psalm 44:24
[a]Job 13:24; Ps 88:14
[b]Ps 42:9; Lam 5:20

Psalm 44:25
[a]Ps 119:25

Psalm 44:26
[a]Ps 35:2
[b]Ps 6:4; 25:22

Targum

Psa. 44:1 For praise; for David, composed by the sons of Korah, good discernment. [2] O LORD, with our ears we have heard, our fathers have told us of the deed you did in their days, in the days of old. [3] You drove out the Canaanite Gentiles with your mighty hand; and you planted them, the house of Israel, in their land; you broke the peoples and sent them away. [4] For they did not inherit the land by the strength of their swords, and the might of their arms did not redeem them, for [it was] your right hand, and your strong arm and the light of your glorious splendor; for whenever they occupied themselves with the Torah, you were pleased with them. [5] You are my king, O God; at this time command the redemption of the house of Jacob. [6] At your command we will gore our oppressors; in your name we will subdue all who rise against us. [7] For I do not trust in my bow, and my sword will not redeem me. [8] For you have redeemed us from our oppressors and from those who hate us, you have brought shame upon them. [9] By the word of the LORD we sing praise all day; and your name we will confess forever and ever. [10] Only you have neglected [us] and put us to shame; and your presence will not abide with our forces. [11] You have made us turn our back in the presence of our enemies, and those who hate us have subdued us. [12] You have handed us over like sheep for food, and you have scattered us among the Gentiles. [13] You sold your people for nothing, for no money; and you did not increase property by their exchange. [14] You have made us a disgrace to our neighbors, a mockery and scandal to our surroundings. [15] You have made us a proverb among the Gentiles, a shaking of the head among the nations. [16] All the day my disgrace is before me, and shame has covered my face. [17] From the sound of the reviler and vilifier, from the presence of the enemy and revenge-taker; [18] All this has come upon us, yet we have not neglected you, and we have not been false to your covenant. [19] We will not turn back hesitating, our hearts being proud, but you have diverted our steps from the straightness of the path. [20] For you have humbled us in a place of jackals, and you have covered us with the shadow of death. [21] If we have neglected the name of our God and spread our hands in prayer to an idol of foreign nations – [22] Truly, God will search this out, for he knows the hidden things of the heart. [23] For on your account we are killed all the day; we are accounted as sheep handed over for slaughter. [24] Act mightily; why will you be like a sleeping man, O LORD? Arouse yourself, do not forever be forgetful. [25] Why will you remove your glorious presence, why neglect our shame and oppression? [26] For our soul is bent to the dust; our bowels cleave to the bottom of the pit. [27] Arise, help us, and redeem us, for the sake of your goodness.

Spiritual Awareness

The spiritual rewrite for the verses is in bold.

Introduction

This is the third composition of the sons of Korah. It is a memoir dedicated to Eretz Israel. The Psalm describes vividly the Divine assistance which allowed Israel to conquer the land. Through the study of the Torah and the performance of the mitzvot in the Torah, Israel seized the spiritual cone of each objective in the LORD's plan. The conquest of the land can be seen as a metaphor for Israel conquering the meaning and purpose of the Torah. The Psalmist mourn the bitter defeat that came with the Babylonian Exile because the people abandoned their divine weapons (Torah study). Even in Exile, there was the hope that the LORD would allow a remnant to return to the land.

Superscript

The Psalmist commences this Psalm with a call to the Sefirah Netzach for victory. The NASB translation, along with many of the English translations, use the translation of "choir director" for the word לַמְנַצֵּחַ, which is at its root Netzach.

To the Sefirah Netzach who grants victory

Verse one

Why does Israel have faith in the LORD? The reason is that the Jewish religion is based upon the tradition of our ancestors (fathers), who have told us of what they have experienced. They saw the great acts of the LORD to create and save the nation.

God, we have heard with our ears; our fathers have told us the work you had wrought in their days, in antiquity.

Verse two

The Psalmist gives credit to the hand of the LORD for driving the people out of the Promised Land when Joshua and Israel conquered the land. It was a divine judgment that the LORD gave to the tribes in the land that resisted Israel.

With your hand, you drove out the nations through the Sefirah Gevurah and drove them away.

Verse three

כִּי לֹא בְחַרְבָּם (key lo v'char'bam) – means "because of their swords." The Israelites owned the possession of the land to three factors. First is that the LORD's right hand saved them. Secondly, the LORD's arm chastised the Canaanites. The third is the bliss inherent in the goals of Divine sovereignty.

For not by their own sword have they conquered the land, their arm has not saved them, but it was Your right hand and Your arm and the light of Your countenance because You found Your will in them.

Verse four

The Psalmist said that the LORD intervened with acts that revealed You in their early history.

You are my king, even as You are God, executing judgment. Commanding the salvation of Jacob.

Verses five & six

The Psalmist says that the LORD's aid overcame the oppressors even while Israel was in exile. Through the LORD's name, Israel's foes were driven off.

With You, we would push down our oppressors, and with Your Name, we would tread them under that which rises up against us.

For I would not put my trust in my bow, neither should my sword save me.

Verse seven

The people experienced the LORD's help while in exile in Babylon.

For You have saved us from our oppressors, and You have put to shame those who sowed hatred against us.

Verse eight

בֵּאלֹהִים (bealohim) – means "in God." This was the motto with which Israel has always confidently faced the future. Israel gratefully recorded every new acquisition and will always give thanks to the Name of the LORD alone forever.

In God, this was our glory all the day, and we shall give thanks to Your Name forever. Meditate on this verse.

Verse nine

During the Babylonian Exile, the Hebrew people felt that the LORD was not with them. In Exile, the Israelites prayed to the LORD, telling Him that they never forgot Him.

Even though You seemed to forget us while we were in Exile, you did make us aware of our unworthiness, and you did go out with our armies.

Verse ten

The Israelites knew that they were powerless because the LORD was not with their armies. They could not fight back. The hatred of the surrounding nations was caused by slander and because of the selfishness of those nations.

You make us turn back when an enemy appears, and those who sow hatred against us plunder us for their own gains.

Verse eleven

The Hebrew people believed that to murder a Jew, in that time, seemed no more wicked than to slaughter a sheep. The people wondered why the LORD allowed the murdering of His people to occur. Eventually, the Hebrew people were scattered and became minorities in foreign countries.

You give us up like sheep to be murdered and have scattered us among the nations.

Verse twelve

The people felt that they were like property of the LORD. The people saw how different nations conquered them to rule over them. The LORD did not earn profit by doing this. Thus, it was difficult to understand why it was happening.

You sell Your people for worthless gain and have truly had no gain from their constant exchanges.

Verse thirteen

The people around us know that our life with you, LORD is a great way to live.

You make us an object of ridicule to our neighbors, a scorn and derision to those around us.

Verse fourteen

The surrounding nations laughed at Israel.

You have made a joke around the nations, a laughingstock among the peoples.

Verses fifteen & sixteen

The nation felt that they were covered in shame.

All-day long, my dishonor is before me, and my humiliation has overwhelmed me,

Before the voice of him, that reviles and blasphemes, before the enemy and the avenger.

Verse seventeen

All that came upon Israel (verse 9-16) led the people to determine that the covenant with the LORD might have been broken.

All this came upon us, but yet we have not forgotten You; we have not been false to Your covenant.

Verses eighteen & nineteen

תַּנִּי (tanee) – means "dragon or sea monster." The NASB translation uses the word jackals which is incorrect.

The Psalmist uses the excuse that the breaking of the covenant from time to time was caused by the suffering of the violence against Israel. It became too much for the people.

Our hearts had not turned back, even when our steps turned away from Your path.

When You allowed us to be trodden down where dragons dwell and covered us with the shadow of death.

Verses twenty and twenty-one

When our actions demonstrated a lack of adherence to the LORD's Torah, the people never forgot the LORD. In history, the circumstances of that time forced the people to act against the LORD. It was an unfortunate time for both the LORD and Israel.

Had we forgotten the Name of our God, even when we spread forth our hands to a strange god,

Then God would search this out, for he knows the heart's secrets.

Verse twenty-two

The Psalmist said to the LORD that despite what looked like disloyalty, the people did demonstrate at times that they were killing and ready to die for the LORD like slaughtered sheep.

For it was for Your sake that we were killed all this time; we were considered sheep for the slaughter.

Verses twenty-three & twenty-four

Even though it appears that LORD, you are asleep, we still call out to your Name.

Show that You are awake; why do you wish to appear as if asleep, LORD? Let it be a time of waking; forsake us not forever

Why do You wish to hide your countenance and forget our affliction and oppression?

Verse twenty-six

Both the LORD and Israel have lost our mental and physical power to rise again.

For our soul is bowed down to the dust; our body lies on the ground altogether.

Verse twenty-seven

The Psalmist asks the LORD to come to Israel's aid and redeem her through the Sefirah Chesed.

Arise to our aid, and redeem us through the Sefirah Chesed.

Complete Psalm Rewrite Emphasizing Spiritual Awareness

To the Sefirah Netzach who grants victory

God, we have heard with our ears; our fathers have told us the work you had wrought in their days, in antiquity.

With your hand, you drove out the nations through the Sefirah Gevurah and drove them away.

For not by their own sword have they conquered the land, their arm has not saved them, but it was Your right hand and Your arm and the light of Your countenance because You found Your will in them.

You are my king, even as You are God, executing judgment. Commanding the salvation of Jacob.

With You, we would push down our oppressors, and with Your Name, we would tread them under that which rises up against us.

For I would not put my trust in my bow, neither should my sword save me.

For You have saved us from our oppressors, and You have put to shame those who sowed hatred against us.

In God, this was our glory all the day, and we shall give thanks to Your Name forever. Meditate on this verse.

Even though You seemed to forget us while we were in Exile, you did make us aware of our unworthiness, and you did go out with our armies.

You make us turn back when an enemy appears, and those who sow hatred against us plunder us for their own gains.

You give us up like sheep to be murdered and have scattered us among the nations.

You sell Your people for worthless gain and have truly had no gain from their constant exchanges.

You make us an object of ridicule to our neighbors, a scorn and derision to those around us.

You have made a joke around the nations, a laughingstock among the peoples.

All-day long, my dishonor is before me, and my humiliation has overwhelmed me,

Before the voice of him, that reviles and blasphemes, before the enemy and the avenger.

All this came upon us, but yet we have not forgotten You; we have not been false to Your covenant.

Our hearts had not turned back, even when our steps turned away from Your path.

When You allowed us to be trodden down where dragons dwell and covered us with the shadow of death.

Had we forgotten the Name of our God, even when we spread forth our hands to a strange god,

Then God would search this out, for he knows the heart's secrets.

Show that You are awake; why do you wish to appear as if asleep, LORD? Let it be a time of waking; forsake us not forever

Why do You wish to hide your countenance and forget our affliction and oppression?

For our soul is bowed down to the dust; our body lies on the ground altogether.

Arise to our aid, and redeem us through the Sefirah Chesed.

Psalm 45

New American Standard 1995	Hebrew

Psa. 45:0 For the choir director; according to the †Shoshannim. A °Maskil of the sons of Korah. A Song of Love.
 	
Psa. 45:1 My heart [1]overflows with a good theme;
    I [2]address my [3]verses to the [4]King;
    My tongue is the pen of [a]a ready writer.
[2]   You are fairer than the sons of men;
    [a]Grace is poured [1]upon Your lips;
    Therefore God has [b]blessed You forever.
 	
Psa. 45:3 Gird [a]Your sword on *Your* thigh, O [1b]Mighty One,
    In Your splendor and Your majesty!
[4]   And in Your majesty ride on victoriously,
    For the cause of truth and [a]meekness *and* righteousness;
    Let Your [b]right hand teach You [1]awesome things.
[5]   Your [a]arrows are sharp;
    The [b]peoples fall under You;
    Your arrows are [c]in the heart of the King's enemies.
 	
Psa. 45:6 [a]Your throne, O God, is forever and ever;
    A scepter of [b]uprightness is the scepter of Your kingdom.
[7]   You have [a]loved righteousness and hated wickedness;
	לַמְנַצֵּחַ עַל־שֹׁשַׁנִּים **Psa. 45:1**
	לִבְנֵי־קֹרַח מַשְׂכִּיל שִׁיר
	יְדִידֹת: ‏2 רָחַשׁ לִבִּי ׀
	דָּבָר טוֹב אֹמֵר אָנִי מַעֲשַׂי
	לְמֶלֶךְ לְשׁוֹנִי עֵט ׀ סוֹפֵר
	מָהִיר: ‏3 יָפְיָפִיתָ מִבְּנֵי
	אָדָם הוּצַק חֵן בְּשְׂפְתוֹתֶיךָ
	עַל־כֵּן בֵּרַכְךָ אֱלֹהִים
	לְעוֹלָם: ‏4 חֲגוֹר־חַרְבְּךָ
	עַל־יָרֵךְ גִּבּוֹר הוֹדְךָ
	וַהֲדָרֶךָ: ‏5 וַהֲדָרְךָ ׀ צְלַח
	רְכַב עַל־דְּבַר־אֱמֶת
	וְעַנְוָה־צֶדֶק וְתוֹרְךָ
	נוֹרָאוֹת יְמִינֶךָ: ‏6 חִצֶּיךָ
	שְׁנוּנִים עַמִּים תַּחְתֶּיךָ
	יִפְּלוּ בְּלֵב אוֹיְבֵי הַמֶּלֶךְ:
	‏7 כִּסְאֲךָ אֱלֹהִים עוֹלָם
	וָעֶד שֵׁבֶט מִישֹׁר שֵׁבֶט
	מַלְכוּתֶךָ: ‏8 אָהַבְתָּ צֶּדֶק

Therefore God, Your God, has [b]anointed You

With the oil of joy above Your fellows.

8 All Your garments are *fragrant with* [a]myrrh and aloes *and* cassia;

Out of ivory palaces [b]stringed instruments have made You glad.

9 Kings' daughters are among [a]Your noble ladies;

At Your [b]right hand stands the queen in [c]gold from Ophir.

Psa. 45:10 Listen, O daughter, give attention and incline your ear:

[a]Forget your people and your father's house;

11 Then the King will desire your beauty.

Because He is your [a]Lord, [b]bow down to Him.

12 The daughter of [a]Tyre *will come* with a gift;

The [b]rich among the people will seek your favor.

Psa. 45:13 The King's daughter is all glorious within;

Her clothing is [a]interwoven with gold.

14 She will be [a]led to the King [b]in embroidered work;

The [c]virgins, her companions who follow her,

Will be brought to You.

15 They will be led forth with gladness and rejoicing;

They will enter into the King's palace.

וַתִּשְׂנָא רֶשַׁע עַל־כֵּן |
מְשָׁחֲךָ אֱלֹהִים אֱלֹהֶיךָ
9 : שֶׁמֶן שָׂשׂוֹן מֵחֲבֵרֶיךָ
מֹר־וַאֲהָלוֹת קְצִיעוֹת כָּל־
בִּגְדֹתֶיךָ מִן־הֵיכְלֵי שֵׁן
מִנִּי שִׂמְּחוּךָ : 10 בְּנוֹת
מְלָכִים בְּיִקְּרוֹתֶיךָ נִצְּבָה
שֵׁגַל לִימִינְךָ בְּכֶתֶם
אוֹפִיר : 11 שִׁמְעִי־בַת וּרְאִי
וְהַטִּי אָזְנֵךְ וְשִׁכְחִי עַמֵּךְ
וּבֵית אָבִיךְ : 12 וְיִתְאָו
הַמֶּלֶךְ יָפְיֵךְ כִּי־הוּא
אֲדֹנַיִךְ וְהִשְׁתַּחֲוִי־לוֹ : 13
וּבַת־צֹר | בְּמִנְחָה פָּנַיִךְ
יְחַלּוּ עֲשִׁירֵי עָם : 14 כָּל־
כְּבוּדָּה בַת־מֶלֶךְ פְּנִימָה
מִמִּשְׁבְּצוֹת זָהָב לְבוּשָׁהּ :
15 לִרְקָמוֹת תּוּבַל לַמֶּלֶךְ
בְּתוּלוֹת אַחֲרֶיהָ רֵעוֹתֶיהָ
מוּבָאוֹת לָךְ : 16 תּוּבַלְנָה
בִּשְׂמָחֹת וָגִיל תְּבֹאֶינָה

Psa. 45:16   In place of your fathers will be your sons;

You shall make them princes in all the earth.

[17]   I will cause *"Your name to be remembered in all generations;

Therefore the peoples *b*will give You thanks forever and ever.

בְּהֵיכַל מֶלֶךְ ׃ 17 תַּחַת
אֲבֹתֶיךָ יִהְיוּ בָנֶיךָ
תְּשִׁיתֵמוֹ לְשָׂרִים בְּכָל־
הָאָרֶץ ׃ 18 אַזְכִּירָה שִׁמְךָ
בְּכָל־דֹּר וָדֹר עַל־כֵּן
עַמִּים יְהוֹדֻךָ לְעֹלָם וָעֶד ׃

References

Psalm 45:1
[1]Lit *is astir*
[2]Lit *am saying*
[3]Lit *works*
[4]Probably refers to Solomon as a type of Christ
[a]Ezra 7:6

Psalm 45:2
[1]Or *through*
[a]Luke 4:22
[b]Ps 21:6

Psalm 45:3
[1]Or *warrior*
[a]Heb 4:12; Rev 1:16
[b]Is 9:6

Psalm 45:4
[1]Or *fearful*
[a]Zeph 2:3
[b]Ps 21:8

Psalm 45:5
[a]Ps 18:14; 120:4; Is 5:28; 7:13
[b]Ps 92:9
[c]2 Sam 18:14

Psalm 45:6
[a]Ps 93:2; Heb 1:8, 9
[b]Ps 98:9

Psalm 45:7
[a]Ps 11:7; 33:5
[b]Ps 2:2

Psalm 45:8
[a]Song 4:14; John 19:39
[b]Ps 150:4

Psalm 45:9
[a]Song 6:8
[b]1 Kin 2:19
[c]1 Kin 9:28; Is 13:12

Psalm 45:10
[a]Deut 21:13; Ruth 1:16, 17

Psalm 45:11
[a]Gen 18:12; 1 Pet 3:6
[b]Eph 5:33

Psalm 45:12
[a]Ps 87:4
[b]Ps 22:29; 68:29; 72:10, 11; Is 49:23

Psalm 45:13
[a]Ex 39:2, 3

Psalm 45:14
[a]Song 1:4
[b]Judg 5:30; Ezek 16:10
[c]Ps 45:9

Psalm 45:17
[a]Mal 1:11
[b]Ps 138:4

Targum

Psa. 45:1 For praise; concerning those who sit in the Sanhedrin of Moses, which was spoken in prophecy by the sons of Korah; a good lesson, and a psalm, and a thanksgiving. **2** My heart desires fine speech; I will speak my work to the king; the utterance of my tongue is quick, like the pen of a fluent scribe. **3** Your beauty, O King Messiah, is greater than the sons of men; the spirit of prophecy has been placed on your lips; because of this the LORD has blessed you forever. **4** Gird your sword on your thigh, O champion; your glory and your brilliance is to kill kings as well as rulers. **5** And your brilliance is great; therefore you will succeed in mounting the horse of the kingdom, by reason of faithfulness and truth and humility and righteousness; and the LORD will teach you to do fearful things with your right hand. **6** Your arrows are drawn to kill Gentile hordes; beneath you they will fall; and the sons of your bow will be released into the heart of the enemies of the king. **7** The throne of your glory, O LORD, lasts forever and ever; the scepter of your kingdom is an upright scepter. **8** Because you have loved righteousness and hated wickedness – because of this the LORD your God has anointed you with the oil of gladness more than your fellows. **9** Pure myrrh and aloe-wood and cassia – your garments are perfected, from the palaces paved with ivory below; from me they will make you glad. **10** The provinces of the kingdom come to welcome you and to honor you, while the book of Torah is stationed at your right side, and written in gold from Ophir. **11** Hear, O congregation of Israel, the Torah of his mouth, and see the wonders of his deeds, and incline your ear to the words of Torah, and you will forget the evil deeds of the wicked of your people, and the place of idols that you worshipped in the house of your father. **12** And then the king will desire your beauty; for he is your master and you will bow down to him. **13** And those who dwell in the fortress of Tyre will come with an offering, and the rich Gentiles will seek your face at your sanctuary. **14** All the best and choicest sacrifices from the provinces, the treasuries of the kings that are hidden within, will they bring for the priests whose clothing is chased with pure gold. **15** In their decorated garments they will offer their sacrifices before the king of the world, and the rest of their fellows who are scattered among the Gentiles will be brought in joy to you to Jerusalem. **16** They will be brought in joy and praise and they will enter the temple of the king of ages. **17** In the place of your fathers will be the righteous, your sons; you will appoint them as leaders in all the land. **18** At that time you will say, "We will invoke your name in every generation"; because of this the Gentiles who are converted will praise your name forever and ever and ever.

Spiritual Awareness

The spiritual rewrite for the verses is in bold.

Introduction & Superscript

This Psalm is seen as a song of praise for the Sages of the Sanhedrin of Moses and was composed prophetically by the sons of Korach. This explanation comes from the Targum. The Sages are the interpreters of the Torah who lived in the latter years before Yeshua and for a few years after. Korach was the person who led a failed rebellion against Moses (can be found in Numbers 16:2). The sons of Korach at first helped their father but later on decided that their father was wrong. The sons turned on their father and supported Moses.

The Torah scholar resembles a rose. This is a delicate flower surrounded by thorns. The thorns seem ready to pierce the flower's delegate petals. But instead, the thorns protect the petals.

The Midrash for this Psalm equates it to Abraham, David, and the Messiah. Each was first rejected by people and later accepted.

Rabbi Hirsch explains the Psalm as a wedding song celebrating the marriage of a bride and groom. Arranged marriages bring together two people who do not know each other well. Conflicts occur at the beginning of the marriage as the couple learns about each other. Eventually, they learn to love each other. Hirsch's explanation fit the ideas of the Midrash. Abraham was chastised for spreading his belief in a single all-powerful

God. Still, he was eventually accepted, and his people became the Jewish nation. David was vilified and pursued by Saul. After a civil war, David became the most beloved King of Israel. The Midrash says that the Messiah will arrive and be challenged before acceptance.

The Psalmist calls out to the Sefirah Netzach for victory.

To Him who grants victory, upon the roses, by the sons of Korach, an instruction, a song of friendship.

Verse one

Ordinary writers search for pretty words that would express an emotion. The Korachite's source was not in their heads but rather in their hearts. Thus this song was fully formed within the author's heart. The words serve only to utter that which the heart has created. The tongue is merely the stenographer's pen which allows the notes of the song to be written down.

My heart has given me this song which I now utter to a king; my tongue will utter the words so the pen can write them down.

Verse two

People can see that you are not ordinary. The LORD has appointed you to such a high calling. The Psalmist does not glorify the royal crown. He glorifies the attributes that are a part of a king's personality and would distinguish him from other men even if he were not a king.

You are fairer than ordinary men; grace is poured upon your lips; therefore, God has blessed you forever.

Verse three

The sword at your side is not for decoration. It symbolizes your majesty because you wield it as a hero.

Gird your sword around your thigh, O mighty one; it is your majesty and ornament.

Verse four

This person employs the service of the cause of truth and right in their life.

But this is your true glory; process and wield guidance for the cause of truth and the championless right; then your right hand will teach you amazing things.

Verse five

The preceding verses describe the usage of royal power in peacetime. When this is done for the service of truth, the arrows become the weapon of victory against the king's enemies.

Your arrows are sharp; The people fall under you; Those who are the king's foes have the arrows piercing their hearts.

Verse six

This verse recognizes that the LORD is the ruler of the Earth forever.

Your throne, God is forever and ever because the scepter of equity is the scepter of your kingdom.

Verse seven

What makes the LORD different from the false gods and idols is that the LORD loves righteousness and hates evil. Evil must be eliminated because it is an obstacle to the exercise and cultivation of all that is good.

You love righteousness by hating lawlessness; therefore, God, your God, has anointed you with gladsome consecration above your fellows.

Verse eight

The fragrances on the garments can be smelt. The odor comes from the fragrant trees making the king glad.

With myrrh and aloes, and cassia are all in your garments, from the ivory palaces (towers) which gladdened you.

Verse nine

The king's daughters are present to participate in the wedding feast.

King's daughters are among Your noble ladies; at your right-hand stands the queen in gold jewelry of Ophir.

Verse ten

The Psalmist tells the ladies to give their attention to what they see and hear. They are to dismiss from their mind any thoughts that make them sad.

Hearken, O daughter and see, incline your ear and forget your own kinfolk and your father's house.

Verse eleven

The Psalmist tells the ladies not to grieve because sadness can affect their beauty.

So that the king shall rejoice in your beauty, for he is your master, and bow down to him.

Verse twelve

A delegation from Tyre will come to pay homage to the ladies.

The daughter of Tyre will come with a gift; the rich among the people will seek your favor.

Verse thirteen

The princess may appear glorious and splendid in public. She only reveals her true glory in womanly virtue in a quiet, more private circle. Her inner beauty outshines her outer beauty.

But the King's daughter is all glorious within, more than in the golden borders of her attire.

Verse fourteen

She comes before the king in the most beautiful clothing.

She is brought to embroideries only for the sake of the king; the maidens who attend her are her friends. They are led to you.

Verse fifteen

They are led with gladness and rejoicing; they enter the palace of the king.

Verse sixteen

The joy of being a parent is that one of the daughters' sons will become king.

May your sons step into the palace of your fathers; may you appoint them as princes in all the lands.

Verse seventeen

I will cause your name to be remembered in all generations; therefore, the people will give you thanks forever and ever.

Complete Psalm Rewrite Emphasizing Spiritual Awareness

To Him who grants victory, upon the roses, by the sons of Korach, an instruction, a song of friendship.

My heart has given me this song which I now utter to a king; my tongue will utter the words so the pen can write them down.

You are fairer than ordinary men; grace is poured upon your lips; therefore, God has blessed you forever.

Gird your sword around your thigh, O mighty one; it is your majesty and ornament.

But this is your true glory; process and wield guidance for the cause of truth and the championless right; then your right hand will teach you amazing things.

Your arrows are sharp; The people fall under you; Those who are the king's foes have the arrows piercing their hearts.

Your throne, God is forever and ever because the scepter of equity is the scepter of your kingdom.

You love righteousness by hating lawlessness; therefore, God, your God, has anointed you with gladsome consecration above your fellows.

With myrrh and aloes, and cassia are all in your garments, from the ivory palaces (towers) which gladdened you.

King's daughters are among Your noble ladies; at your right-hand stands the queen in gold jewelry of Ophir.

Hearken, O daughter and see, incline your ear and forget your own kinfolk and your father's house.

So that the king shall rejoice in your beauty, for he is your master, and bow down to him.

The daughter of Tyre will come with a gift; the rich among the people will seek your favor.

The daughter of Tyre will come with a gift; the rich among the people will seek your favor.

But the King's daughter is all glorious within, more than in the golden borders of her attire.

She is brought to embroideries only for the sake of the king; the maidens who attend her are her friends. They are led to you.

They are led with gladness and rejoicing; they enter the palace of the king.

May your sons step into the palace of your fathers; may you appoint them as princes in all the lands.

I will cause your name to be remembered in all generations; therefore, the people will give you thanks forever and ever.

Psalm 46

New American Standard 1995	Hebrew

Psa. 46:0   For the choir director. *A Psalm* of the sons of Korah, [†]set to Alamoth. A Song.

Psa. 46:1   God is our [a]refuge and strength,
      [1]A very [b]present help [c]in [2]trouble.
[2]   Therefore we will [a]not fear, though [b]the Earth should change
      And though [c]the mountains slip into the heart of the [1]sea;
[3]   Though its [a]waters roar *and* foam,
      Though the mountains quake at its swelling pride.   [1]Selah.

Psa. 46:4   There is a [a]river whose streams make glad the [b]city of God,
      The holy [c]dwelling places of the Most High.
[5]   God is [a]in the midst of her, she will not be moved;
      God will [b]help her [1]when morning dawns.
[6]   The [1]nations [a]made an uproar, the kingdoms tottered;
      He [2b]raised His voice, the Earth [c]melted.
[7]   The LORD of hosts [a]is with us;
      The God of Jacob is [b]our stronghold. Selah.

Psa. 46:8   Come, [a]behold the works of the LORD,
      [1]Who has wrought [b]desolations in the Earth.
[9]   He [a]makes wars to cease to the end of the Earth;

Psa. 46:1 לַמְנַצֵּחַ לִבְנֵי־קֹרַח עַל־עֲלָמוֹת שִׁיר : ‎[2] אֱלֹהִים לָנוּ מַחֲסֶה וָעֹז עֶזְרָה בְצָרוֹת נִמְצָא מְאֹד : ‎[3] עַל־כֵּן לֹא־נִירָא בְּהָמִיר אָרֶץ וּבְמוֹט הָרִים בְּלֵב יַמִּים : ‎[4] יֶהֱמוּ יֶחְמְרוּ מֵימָיו יִרְעֲשׁוּ־הָרִים בְּגַאֲוָתוֹ סֶלָה : ‎[5] נָהָר פְּלָגָיו יְשַׂמְּחוּ עִיר־אֱלֹהִים קְדֹשׁ מִשְׁכְּנֵי עֶלְיוֹן : ‎[6] אֱלֹהִים בְּקִרְבָּהּ בַּל־תִּמּוֹט יַעְזְרֶהָ אֱלֹהִים לִפְנוֹת בֹּקֶר : ‎[7] הָמוּ גוֹיִם מָטוּ מַמְלָכוֹת נָתַן בְּקוֹלוֹ תָּמוּג אָרֶץ : ‎[8] יְהוָה צְבָאוֹת עִמָּנוּ מִשְׂגָּב־לָנוּ אֱלֹהֵי יַעֲקֹב סֶלָה : ‎[9] לְכוּ־חֲזוּ מִפְעֲלוֹת יְהוָה אֲשֶׁר־שָׂם שַׁמּוֹת בָּאָרֶץ : ‎[10] מַשְׁבִּית מִלְחָמוֹת עַד־קְצֵה הָאָרֶץ קֶשֶׁת יְשַׁבֵּר וְקִצֵּץ חֲנִית עֲגָלוֹת יִשְׂרֹף בָּאֵשׁ : ‎[11] הַרְפּוּ וּדְעוּ כִּי־אָנֹכִי אֱלֹהִים אָרוּם בַּגּוֹיִם אָרוּם בָּאָרֶץ : ‎[12] יְהוָה

He [b]breaks the bow and cuts the spear in two; He [c]burns the chariots with fire. 10 "[1]Cease *striving* and [a]know that I am God; I will be [b]exalted among the [2]nations, I will be exalted in the earth." 11 The LORD of hosts is with us; The God of Jacob is our stronghold. Selah.	צְבָא֫וֹת עִמָּ֥נוּ מִשְׂגָּֽב־לָ֥נוּ אֱלֹהֵ֖י יַעֲקֹ֣ב סֶֽלָה׃

References

<table>
<tr><td valign="top" width="50%">

Psalm 46:1
[1]Or *Abundantly available for help*
[2]Or *tight places*
[a]Ps 14:6; 62:7, 8
[b]Deut 4:7; Ps 145:18
[c]Ps 9:9

Psalm 46:2
[1]Lit *seas*
[a]Ps 23:4; 27:1
[b]Ps 82:5
[c]Ps 18:7

Psalm 46:3
[1]*Selah* may mean: *Pause, Crescendo* or *Musical interlude*
[a]Ps 93:3, 4; Jer 5:22

Psalm 46:4
[a]Ps 36:8; 65:9; Is 8:6; Rev 22:1
[b]Ps 48:1; 87:3; 101:8; Is 60:14; Rev 3:12
[c]Ps 43:3

Psalm 46:5
[1]Lit *at the turning of the morning*
[a]Deut 23:14; Is 12:6; Ezek 43:7, 9; Hos 11:9; Joel 2:27; Zech 2:5
[b]Ps 37:40; Is 41:14; Luke 1:54

Psalm 46:6
[1]Or *Gentiles*
[2]Lit *gave forth*
[a]Ps 2:1, 2
[b]Ps 18:13; 68:33; Jer 25:30; Joel 2:11; Amos 1:2
[c]Amos 9:5; Mic 1:4; Nah 1:5

</td><td valign="top" width="50%">

Psalm 46:7
[a]Num 14:9; 2 Chr 13:12
[b]Ps 9:9; 48:3

Psalm 46:8
[1]Or *Which He has wrought as desolations*
[a]Ps 66:5
[b]Is 61:4; Jer 51:43

Psalm 46:9
[a]Is 2:4; Mic 4:3
[b]1 Sam 2:4; Ps 76:3
[c]Is 9:5; Ezek 39:9

Psalm 46:10
[1]Or *Let go, relax*
[2]Or *Gentiles*
[a]Ps 100:3
[b]Is 2:11, 17

</td></tr>
</table>

Targum

Psa. 46:1 For praise, by the sons of Korah, through the spirit of prophecy when their father was hidden from them, but they were saved, and they recited this song. **2** God is for us security and strength; a help in distress we shall find indeed. **3** Because of this we will not be afraid in the time our fathers passed from the land, when the mountains totter in the depth of the great sea. **4** His waters shake, they become muddy from their dust; the mountains tremble in your pride forever. **5** Peoples like rivers and their fountains come and make glad the city of the LORD, and they pray in the LORD's sanctuary, his exalted dwelling. **6** The presence of the LORD is within it, it will not be shaken; the LORD will help her for the merit of Abraham who prayed on it at the morning hours. **7** When the Torah was given to his people, the Gentiles trembled; kingdoms shook when he raised his voice; and when he gave the Torah to his people, the inhabitants of the Earth melted. **8** The word of the LORD Sabaoth is our help; the God of Jacob is a stronghold for us forever. **9** Come, see the deeds of the LORD who has put devastation on the wicked of the land. **10** He annuls war to the ends of the Earth; he will break the bow and shatter the lance; the round shields he will burn with fire. **11** Cease from war, and know that I am the LORD, exalted among the peoples, exalted over the inhabitants of the Earth. **12** The word of the LORD Sabaoth is our help; the God of Jacob is a stronghold for us forever.

Spiritual Awareness

The spiritual rewrite for the verses is in bold.

Introduction and Superscript

This psalm was authored by the sons of Korach after their father disappeared before their eyes. The LORD delivered Korach's sons from the Earth, which opened up and threatened to swallow them with their father. The LORD delivered Korach's sons with divine salvation. The sons foresaw the future where Israel was threatened and damaged by foreign armies and by cataclysms.

The psalm's title alludes to the many worlds thus indicating that the LORD's salvation is expressed constantly throughout the world.

עֲלָמוֹת שִׁיר (alamot sheer) – means "a song to the maiden." The phrase is an idiom meaning "the mysteries of life" which are hidden to most people but can be sensed in the ecstasy of song. *Alamot* was the name of a musical instrument that women played.

Israel owes its current and future good fortune to the LORD. This psalm is directed to the Sefirah Netzach.

To Him who grants victory, by the sons of Korach, upon the mysteries of son.

Verse one

Remember to place your full trust in the LORD for the present and the future.

God is our trust and strength, a ready helper in times of trouble.

Verse two

Israel would not fear what was happening on the Earth even when it is undergoing violent change. Why? Because Israel places its trust in the LORD to take care of them.

God is our trust and strength, a ready helper in times of trouble.
occurs, which moves mountains into the midst of the seas.

Verse three

Israel will not be afraid because she will see the LORD's hand in the midst of catastrophes. Meditate upon the verse.

Though its waters roar and foam, though the mountains quake at its swelling pride. Selah.

Verse four

Even in the violent changes of the Earth there will be one place where things will not be destroyed or damaged. That place is where the Temple was built, the city of Jerusalem.

There is one river; His streams they make glad the city of God, of Him Who is sanctified in the dwelling-places of the Host High.

Verse five

This is just a reminder that the LORD does not only dwell in the Temple in Jerusalem.

God is in this midst, He is everywhere, therefore do not waver. The LORD will help it at the dawn of morning.

Verses six & seven

Perhaps the pagan leaders of the world will see how the LORD affected history. These people may come to know the LORD as the world's leader. Meditate upon this sentence.

Though nations are in anxious tumult, though Kingdoms totter, through His call of thunder has decreed that the Earth shall melt.
The God of hosts is with us; the God of Jacob is our high tower. Selah.

Verse eight

How does the LORD is here? The answer is to look at everything on the Earth.
Come behold the works of the LORD, who made desolations on Earth.

Verse nine

The LORD desires that all wars stop. War destroys the beauty of the Earth.

The LORD makes wars cease until the end of the Earth; He breaks the box and cuts the spear to pieces; He burns the chariots of fire.

Verse ten

The LORD will destroy all the peoples who do worship idols and false gods.

"Detest and know that I am God, exalted among the nations, exalted upon Earth.

Verse eleven

What is our high tower? Ancient cities were built with high walls and a high tower so that lookouts could see if an enemy was approaching. Jerusalem had a tower named "David's tower." When the Assyrians and Babylonians came to the city, a guard in the tower would signal an alarm. Meditate upon this verse,

The LORD is with us; the God of Jacob is our high tower. Selah.

Complete Psalm Rewrite Emphasizing Spiritual Awareness

To Him who grants victory, by the sons of Korach, upon the mysteries of son.

God is our trust and strength, a ready helper in times of trouble.

Though its waters roar and foam, though the mountains quake at its swelling pride. Selah.

God is in this midst, He is everywhere, therefore do not waver. The LORD will help it at the dawn of morning.

Though nations are in anxious tumult, though Kingdoms totter, through His call of thunder has decreed that the Earth shall melt.

The God of hosts is with us; the God of Jacob is our high tower. Selah.

Come behold the works of the LORD, who made desolations on Earth.

The LORD makes wars cease until the end of the Earth; He breaks the box and cuts the spear to pieces; He burns the chariots of fire.

The LORD is with us; the God of Jacob is our high tower. Selah.

Psalm 47

New American Standard 1995	Hebrew
Psa. 47:0 For the choir director. A Psalm of the sons of Korah. **Psa. 47:1** O [a]clap your hands, all peoples; 　[b]Shout to God with the voice of [1]joy. 2　For the LORD Most High is to be [a]feared, 　A [b]great King over all the earth. 3　He [a]subdues peoples under us 　And nations under our feet. 4　He chooses our [a]inheritance for us, 　The [b]glory of Jacob whom He loves. [1]Selah. **Psa. 47:5** God has [a]ascended [1]with a shout, 　The LORD, [1]with the [b]sound of a trumpet. 6　[a]Sing praises to God, sing praises; 　Sing praises to [b]our King, sing praises. 7　For God is the [a]King of all the earth; 　Sing praises [b]with a [1]skillful psalm. 8　God [a]reigns over the nations, 　God [1]sits on [b]His holy throne. 9　The [1a]princes of the people have assembled themselves *as* the [b]people of the God of Abraham, 　For the [c]shields of the earth belong to God; 　He [2]is [d]highly exalted.	לַמְנַצֵּחַ ׀ לִבְנֵי־קֹרַח Psa. 47:1 מִזְמוֹר ׃ ² כָּל־הָעַמִּים תִּקְעוּ־כָף הָרִיעוּ לֵאלֹהִים בְּקוֹל רִנָּה ׃ ³ כִּי־יְהוָה עֶלְיוֹן נוֹרָא מֶלֶךְ גָּדוֹל עַל־כָּל־ הָאָרֶץ ׃ ⁴ יַדְבֵּר עַמִּים תַּחְתֵּינוּ וּלְאֻמִּים תַּחַת רַגְלֵינוּ ׃ ⁵ יַבְחַר־לָנוּ אֶת־ נַחֲלָתֵנוּ אֶת גְּאוֹן יַעֲקֹב אֲשֶׁר־אָהֵב סֶלָה ׃ ⁶ עָלָה אֱלֹהִים בִּתְרוּעָה יְהוָה בְּקוֹל שׁוֹפָר ׃ ⁷ זַמְּרוּ אֱלֹהִים זַמֵּרוּ זַמְּרוּ לְמַלְכֵּנוּ זַמֵּרוּ ׃ ⁸ כִּי מֶלֶךְ כָּל־הָאָרֶץ אֱלֹהִים זַמְּרוּ מַשְׂכִּיל ׃ ⁹ מָלַךְ אֱלֹהִים עַל־גּוֹיִם אֱלֹהִים יָשַׁב ׀ עַל־כִּסֵּא קָדְשׁוֹ ׃ ¹⁰ נְדִיבֵי עַמִּים וְנֶאֶסְפוּ עַם

	אֱלֹהֵי אַבְרָהָם כִּי לֵאלֹהִים מָגִנֵּי־אֶרֶץ מְאֹד נַעֲלָה׃

References

Psalm 47:1 [1]Or *a ringing cry* [a]Ps 98:8 [b]Ps 106:47 **Psalm 47:2** [a]Deut 7:21; Neh 1:5; Ps 66:3, 5; 68:35 [b]Mal 1:14 **Psalm 47:3** [a]Ps 18:47 **Psalm 47:4** [1]*Selah* may mean: *Pause, Crescendo* or *Musical interlude* [a]1 Pet 1:4 [b]Amos 6:8; 8:7; Nah 2:2 **Psalm 47:5** [1]Or *amid* [a]Ps 68:18 [b]Ps 98:6 **Psalm 47:6** [a]Ps 68:4 [b]Ps 89:18 **Psalm 47:7** [1]Heb *Maskil* [a]Zech 14:9 [b]1 Cor 14:15 **Psalm 47:8** [1]Or *has taken His seat* [a]1 Chr 16:31; Ps 22:28 [b]Ps 97:2	**Psalm 47:9** [1]Or *nobles* [2]Lit *has greatly exalted Himself* [a]Ps 72:11; 102:22; Is 49:7, 23 [b]Rom 4:11, 12 [c]Ps 89:18 [d]Ps 97:9

Targum

Psa. 47:1 For praise, by the sons of Korah, a psalm. ² All you peoples, clap hands in joy, shout in the presence of the LORD with the sound of praise. ³ For the LORD Most High is to be feared, a great king over all the earth. ⁴ He will slay the peoples by plague instead of us, and he will subdue the nations under our feet. ⁵ He will favor us to inherit our heritage, the sanctuary of Jacob whom he loves forever. ⁶ Let the LORD be exalted with a shout, the LORD with the sound of the trumpet. ⁷ Sing praise in the presence of the LORD, sing praise; sing praise to our king, sing praise! ⁸ For the LORD is king over all inhabitants of the earth; sing praise before him with good understanding. ⁹ The LORD is king over the peoples; the LORD sits on his holy throne. ¹⁰ The leaders of the Gentiles have gathered, the Gentiles who believe in the God of Abraham, for in the presence of the LORD they are the shields of the earth; he has been greatly exalted.

Spiritual Awareness

The spiritual rewrite for the verses is in bold.

Introduction

This Psalm is a sequel to the previous one, which describes the defeat of the nations who united against the LORD and His chosen people. The ability of the shofar blast to inspire people is a part of this Psalm, and it invokes the LORD's mercy through Chesed. On Rosh Hashannah, this Psalm is recited seven times before the sounding of the shofar.

The sages teach that there are forty-nine levels of spiritual impurity before one reaches the lowest depth of Sheol. Correspondingly there are forty-nine levels of sanctity that one can obtain. Forty-nine times on Rosh Hashannah, the LORD's name is recited, which alludes to the power of this Psalm to transform the forty-nine possible levels of spiritual uncleanliness into the forty-nine corresponding levels of sanctity and purity.[2]

Superscript

This Psalm proclaims how the historical events of Israel inspire all the other nations to do homage to the LORD.

To the Sefirah Netzach, a Psalm by the sons of Korach.

---

[2] https://www.chabad.org/library/article_cdo/aid/3680881/jewish/How-49-and-49-Equal-49.htm. Accessed 5/14/2022.

Verse one

תִּקְעוּ־כָף (teek'oo kaf) – means "clap your hands." This phrase usually refers to a handclasp implying an obligation like giving a promise.

הָרִיעוּ לֵאלֹהִים (hareeoo lealohim) – means "shout to God." This phrase calls for a powerful sound because it refers to the LORD. It also denotes the tribute to the LORD paid by the human spirit deeply moved by the thought of His overwhelming greatness.

Clasp hands, all your peoples, call forth to God the tribute loudly with rejoicing.

Verse Two

The LORD is a great ruler to be revered even as He proves to be near us through the Shekinah. His loving-kindness through the Sefirah Chesed can be found everywhere. Blessings from the LORD come to people who follow His Laws.

For the LORD who loves all things is the Most High and must be revered for all things.

Verses three & four

There is the belief that all the people of the world will eventually come together with the nation of Israel to worship the LORD.

He gathers the people together beneath us and nations under our feet.

He chooses our inheritance for us, the pride of Jacob, which He loves. Meditate upon this verse.

Verse five

The LORD will reveal himself to other nations once those nations have obeyed the summons and once the minds of the countries come to know God. He will then reveal himself to them.

When God has ascended amidst a shout, He will appear as God, all-merciful with the sound of the shofar.

Verses six & seven

Therefore sing, sing praises to God, sing praises to our King, sing praises.

For God is the King of all the earth, sing to spread this knowledge far and wide.

Verses eight and nine

God reigns over the nations; God sits on His holy throne.

The princes of the people have assembled themselves *as* the people of the God of Abraham, For the shields of the earth belong to God; He is highly exalted.

Complete Psalm Rewrite Emphasizing Spiritual Awareness

To the Sefirah Netzach, a Psalm by the sons of Korach.

Clasp hands, all your peoples, call forth to God the tribute loudly with rejoicing.

For the LORD who loves all things is the Most High and must be revered for all things.

He gathers the people together beneath us and nations under our feet.

He chooses our inheritance for us, the pride of Jacob, which He loves. Meditate upon this verse.

Therefore sing, sing praises to God, sing praises to our King, sing praises.

For God is the King of all the earth, sing to spread this knowledge far and wide.

God reigns over the nations; God sits on His holy throne.
The princes of the people have assembled themselves *as* the people of the God of Abraham, For the shields of the earth belong to God; He is highly exalted.

Psalm 48

New American Standard 1995	Hebrew

Psa. 48:0 A Song; a Psalm of the sons of Korah.

Psa. 48:1 [a]"Great is the LORD, and greatly to be praised,

In the [b]city of our God, His [c]holy mountain.

2   [a]Beautiful in elevation, [b]the joy of the whole earth,

Is Mount Zion *in* the far north,

The [c]city of the great King.

3   God, in her palaces,

Has made Himself known as a [a]stronghold.

Psa. 48:4 For, lo, the [a]kings assembled themselves,

They passed by together.

5   They saw *it*, then they were amazed;

They were [a]terrified, they [1]fled in alarm.

6   [1]Panic seized them there,

Anguish, as of [a]a woman in childbirth.

7   With the [a]east wind

You [b]break the [c]ships of Tarshish.

8   As we have heard, so have we seen

In the city of the LORD of hosts, in the city of our God;

God will [a]establish her forever. [1]Selah.

Psa. 48:9 We have thought on [a]Your lovingkindness, O God,

In the midst of Your temple.

Psa. 48:1 שִׁיר מִזְמוֹר לִבְנֵי־

קֹרַח ׃ 2 גָּדוֹל יְהוָה וּמְהֻלָּל

מְאֹד בְּעִיר אֱלֹהֵינוּ הַר־קָדְשׁוֹ ׃

3 יְפֵה נוֹף מְשׂוֹשׂ כָּל־הָאָרֶץ

הַר־צִיּוֹן יַרְכְּתֵי צָפוֹן קִרְיַת

מֶלֶךְ רָב ׃ 4 אֱלֹהִים

בְּאַרְמְנוֹתֶיהָ נוֹדַע לְמִשְׂגָּב ׃ 5

כִּי־הִנֵּה הַמְּלָכִים נוֹעֲדוּ עָבְרוּ

יַחְדָּו ׃ 6 הֵמָּה רָאוּ כֵּן תָּמָהוּ

נִבְהֲלוּ נֶחְפָּזוּ ׃ 7 רְעָדָה אֲחָזָתַם

שָׁם חִיל כַּיּוֹלֵדָה ׃ 8 בְּרוּחַ

קָדִים תְּשַׁבֵּר אֳנִיּוֹת תַּרְשִׁישׁ ׃ 9

כַּאֲשֶׁר שָׁמַעְנוּ ׀ כֵּן רָאִינוּ

בְּעִיר־יְהוָה צְבָאוֹת בְּעִיר

אֱלֹהֵינוּ אֱלֹהִים יְכוֹנְנֶהָ עַד־

עוֹלָם סֶלָה ׃ 10 דִּמִּינוּ אֱלֹהִים

חַסְדֶּךָ בְּקֶרֶב הֵיכָלֶךָ ׃ 11

כְּשִׁמְךָ אֱלֹהִים כֵּן תְּהִלָּתְךָ עַל־

קַצְוֵי־אֶרֶץ צֶדֶק מָלְאָה יְמִינֶךָ ׃

12 יִשְׂמַח ׀ הַר־צִיּוֹן תָּגֵלְנָה

בְּנוֹת יְהוּדָה לְמַעַן מִשְׁפָּטֶיךָ ׃

10 As is Your [a]name, O God,
So is Your [b]praise to the ends of the earth;
Your [c]right hand is full of righteousness.
11 Let Mount [a]Zion be glad,
Let the [a]daughters of Judah rejoice
Because of Your judgments.
12 Walk about Zion and go around her;
Count her [a]towers;
13 Consider her [a]ramparts;
Go through her palaces,
That you may [b]tell *it* to the next generation.
14 For [1]such is God,
Our God forever and ever;
He will [a]guide us [2]until death.

סֹבּוּ צִיּוֹן וְהַקִּיפֻוּהָ סִפְרוּ 13
מִגְדָּלֶיהָ : 14 שִׁיתוּ לִבְּכֶם |
לְחֵילָה פַּסְּגוּ אַרְמְנוֹתֶיהָ לְמַעַן
תְּסַפְּרוּ לְדוֹר אַחֲרוֹן : 15 כִּי זֶה
אֱלֹהִים אֱלֹהֵינוּ עוֹלָם וָעֶד
הוּא יְנַהֲגֵנוּ עַל־מוּת :

References

Psalm 48:1
[a]1 Chr 16:25; Ps 96:4; 145:3
[b]Ps 46:4
[c]Ps 2:6; 87:1; Is 2:3; Mic 4:1; Zech 8:3

Psalm 48:2
[a]Ps 50:2
[b]Lam 2:15
[c]Matt 5:35

Psalm 48:3
[a]Ps 46:7

Psalm 48:4
[a]2 Sam 10:6-19

Psalm 48:5
[1]Lit *were hurried away*
[a]Ex 15:15

Psalm 48:6
[1]Lit *Trembling*
[a]Is 13:8

Psalm 48:7
[a]Jer 18:17
[b]1 Kin 22:48
[c]1 Kin 10:22; Ezek 27:25

Psalm 48:8
[1]*Selah* may mean: *Pause, Crescendo* or *Musical interlude*
[a]Ps 87:5

Psalm 48:9
[a]Ps 26:3; 40:10

Psalm 48:10
[a]Deut 28:58; Josh 7:9; Mal 1:11
[b]Ps 65:1, 2; 100:1
[c]Is 41:10

Psalm 48:11
[a]Ps 97:8

Psalm 48:12
[a]Neh 3:1, 11, 25-27

Psalm 48:13
[a]Ps 122:7
[b]Ps 78:5-7

Psalm 48:14
[1]Lit *this*
[2]Lit *upon;* some mss and the Gr read *forever*
[a]Ps 23:4; Is 58:11

Targum

Psa. 48:1 A song and psalm by the sons of Korah. ² Great is the LORD and very praiseworthy, in Jerusalem, the city of our God, and on the mount of his sanctuary. ³ Beautiful as a bridegroom, the joy of all the inhabitants of the earth, Mount Zion, on the north side, the city of the great king. ⁴ The LORD is in its palaces; it is known for strength. ⁵ For behold, the kings have joined forces, they have passed by together. ⁶ They have seen, so they were amazed at the miracles and wonders; they were astonished, yea, they fled. ⁷ Trembling seized them there, agitation like a woman giving birth. ⁸ With an east wind strong as fire from the presence of the LORD, you will shatter the ships of Tarsis. ⁹ The children of Israel will say, "Just as we have heard, so we have seen; in the city of the LORD Sabaoth, in the city of our God – the LORD will establish it forever and ever." ¹⁰ Make us worthy, O LORD, of your goodness in the midst of your temple. ¹¹ As your name, O LORD, so is your praise to the ends of the earth; your right hand is full of generosity. ¹² Let Mount Zion rejoice, let the assemblies of the house of Judah rejoice with psalms, because of your judgments. ¹³ Surround Zion, let them rejoice, and encircle her, number her towers. ¹⁴ Set your mind on her throngs above, [even on] her citadels, that you may tell it to another generation. ¹⁵ For this, the LORD, he is our God; his presence is in her midst and his dwelling is in heaven forever and ever; he will guide us in the days of our youth.

Spiritual Awareness

The spiritual rewrite for the verses is in bold.

Introduction

The Psalmist describes the future glory of Jerusalem. The rebuilding of the city signals an era of national renewal.

Superscript

A song, a psalm by the sons of Korach

Verse one

"Great is the LORD" is an interesting statement. It indicates that the LORD surpasses every concept humans might have to the power and divine force that rules and shapes the world. What humans cannot do, the LORD can.

Great is the LORD and clearly revealed by His mighty acts in Jerusalem on Mount Zion, His holy mountain.

Verse two

The north of Jerusalem is where the Temple and palaces were located in ancient days.

Beautiful in its view, a joy to all the world. Mount Zion's northern summit, the city of the great King (the LORD).

Verse three

The LORD's greatness is found in other places than just the Temple. The city of Jerusalem with its palaces is one example.

In its palaces, God has been recognized as a stronghold.

Verses four, five, six, and seven

These verses refer to the kings that came together to attack Israel. They grabbed a lot of the land of the Promised land, but they could not take Jerusalem. This sounds like the events when the Assyrians invaded. They were able to seize the land of Judea, but when they got to Jerusalem, the LORD defeated them.

For, lo, the kings assembled themselves, they passed by together.
They saw *it*, then they were amazed; they were terrified, they fled in alarm.
Panic seized them there, anguish, as of a woman in childbirth.
With the east wind, You break the ships of Tarshish.

Verse eight

The greatness of the LORD was told from generation to generation. The psalmist expresses his love for the LORD because he (or they) have experienced the LORD's love for themselves.

Even as we have heard it in the past, so have we seen it now in Jerusalem, the city of the LORD, who established it forever. Meditate on this verse.

Verses nine, ten, and eleven

The name of the LORD brings praises to the wonders and beauty of His creation.

We have thought on Your lovingkindness, O God, in the midst of Your temple.

As is Your name, O God, so is Your praise to the ends of the earth; Your right hand is full of righteousness.

Let Mount Zion be glad, let the daughters of Judah rejoice because of Your judgments.

Verses twelve and thirteen

Israel is called to preserve the city of Jerusalem. They are also charged with proclaiming prosperity that the nation's spiritual, moral, and political soul dwells amid Mount Zion and Jerusalem. This city is the center of Israel.

Rally around Mount Zion, gather around her closely, count her towers,

Set your heart on the circular wall, raise her palaces aloft so that you may tell of it to all future generations.

Verse fourteen

The LORD will lead Israel beyond mortality.

This God is our God forever. He leads us beyond mortality.

Complete Psalm Rewrite Emphasizing Spiritual Awareness

A song, a psalm by the sons of Korach

Great is the LORD and clearly revealed by His mighty acts in Jerusalem on Mount Zion, His holy mountain.

Beautiful in its view, a joy to all the world. Mount Zion's northern summit, the city of the great King (the LORD).

In its palaces, God has been recognized as a stronghold.

For, lo, the kings assembled themselves, they passed by together.

They saw *it,* then they were amazed; they were terrified, they fled in alarm.

Panic seized them there, anguish, as of a woman in childbirth.

With the east wind, You break the ships of Tarshish.

Even as we have heard it in the past, so have we seen it now in Jerusalem, the city of the LORD, who established it forever. Meditate on this verse.

We have thought on Your lovingkindness, O God, in the midst of Your temple.

As is Your name, O God, so is Your praise to the ends of the earth; Your right hand is full of righteousness.

Let Mount Zion be glad, let the daughters of Judah rejoice because of Your judgments.

Rally around Mount Zion, gather around her closely, count her towers,

Set your heart on the circular wall, raise her palaces aloft so that you may tell of it to all future generations.

This God is our God forever. He leads us beyond mortality.

Psalm 49

New American Standard 1995	Hebrew
Psa. 49:0 For the choir director. A Psalm of the sons of Korah.	

Psa. 49:1 [a]Hear this, all peoples;
Give ear, all [b]inhabitants of the world,
2 Both [a]low and high,
Rich and poor together.
3 My mouth will [a]speak wisdom,
And the meditation of my heart *will be* [b]understanding.
4 I will incline my ear to [a]a proverb;
[b]I will [1]express my [c]riddle on the harp.

Psa. 49:5 Why should I [a]fear in days of adversity,
When the iniquity of my [1]foes surrounds me,
6 Even those who [a]trust in their wealth
And boast in the abundance of their riches?
7 No man can by any means [a]redeem *his* brother
Or give to God a [b]ransom for him

—

8 For [a]the redemption of [1]his soul is costly,
And he should cease *trying* forever

—

9 That he should [a]live on eternally,
That he should not [1b]undergo decay.

Psa. 49:10 For he sees *that even* [a]wise men die;

לַמְנַצֵּחַ ׀ וְלִבְנֵי־קֹרַח ‎Psa. 49:1

מִזְמוֹר׃ ‎2 שִׁמְעוּ־זֹאת כָּל־הָעַמִּים הַאֲזִינוּ כָּל־יֹשְׁבֵי

חָלֶד׃ ‎3 גַּם־בְּנֵי אָדָם גַּם־בְּנֵי־אִישׁ יַחַד עָשִׁיר וְאֶבְיוֹן׃

‎4 פִּי יְדַבֵּר חָכְמוֹת וְהָגוּת לִבִּי תְבוּנוֹת׃ ‎5 אַטֶּה לְמָשָׁל אָזְנִי אֶפְתַּח בְּכִנּוֹר חִידָתִי׃

‎6 לָמָּה אִירָא בִּימֵי רָע עֲוֺן עֲקֵבַי יְסוּבֵּנִי׃ ‎7 הַבֹּטְחִים עַל־חֵילָם וּבְרֹב עָשְׁרָם יִתְהַלָּלוּ׃ ‎8 אָח לֹא־פָדֹה יִפְדֶּה אִישׁ לֹא־יִתֵּן לֵאלֹהִים כָּפְרוֹ׃ ‎9 וְיֵקַר פִּדְיוֹן נַפְשָׁם וְחָדַל לְעוֹלָם׃ ‎10 וִיחִי־עוֹד לָנֶצַח לֹא יִרְאֶה הַשָּׁחַת׃ ‎11 כִּי יִרְאֶה ׀ חֲכָמִים יָמוּתוּ יַחַד כְּסִיל וָבַעַר יֹאבֵדוּ וְעָזְבוּ לַאֲחֵרִים חֵילָם׃ ‎12

The *b*stupid and the senseless alike perish

And *c*leave their wealth to others.

11 Their *1a*inner thought is *that* their houses *b*are forever

And their dwelling places to all generations;

They have *c*called their lands after their own names.

12 But *a*man in *his* *1*pomp will not endure;

He is like the *2*beasts that *3*perish.

Psa. 49:13 This is the *a*way of those who are foolish,

And of those after them who *b*approve their words.   *1*Selah.

14 As sheep they are appointed *a*for *1*Sheol;

Death shall be their shepherd;

And the *b*upright shall rule over them in the morning,

And their form shall be for *1*Sheol *c*to consume

*2*So that they have no habitation.

15 But God will *a*redeem my soul from the *1*power of *2*Sheol,

For *b*He will receive me. Selah.

Psa. 49:16 Do not be afraid *a*when a man becomes rich,

When the *1*glory of his house is increased;

17 For when he dies he will *a*carry nothing away;

His *1*glory will not descend after him.

18 Though while he lives he *a*congratulates *1*himself —

And though *men* praise you when you do well for yourself —

קִרְבָּם בָּתֵּימוֹ ׀ לְעוֹלָם מִשְׁכְּנֹתָם לְדֹר וָדֹר קָרְאוּ בִשְׁמוֹתָם עֲלֵי אֲדָמוֹת: 13 וְאָדָם בִּיקָר בַּל־יָלִין נִמְשַׁל כַּבְּהֵמוֹת נִדְמוּ: 14 זֶה דַרְכָּם כֵּסֶל לָמוֹ וְאַחֲרֵיהֶם ׀ בְּפִיהֶם יִרְצוּ סֶלָה: 15 כַּצֹּאן ׀ לִשְׁאוֹל שַׁתּוּ מָוֶת יִרְעֵם וַיִּרְדּוּ בָם יְשָׁרִים ׀ לַבֹּקֶר וְצִירָם [וְ][צוּרָם] לְבַלּוֹת שְׁאוֹל מִזְּבֻל לוֹ: 16 אַךְ־ אֱלֹהִים יִפְדֶּה נַפְשִׁי מִיַּד־ שְׁאוֹל כִּי יִקָּחֵנִי סֶלָה: 17 אַל־תִּירָא כִּי־יַעֲשִׁר אִישׁ כִּי־יִרְבֶּה כְּבוֹד בֵּיתוֹ: 18 כִּי לֹא בְמוֹתוֹ יִקַּח הַכֹּל לֹא־ יֵרֵד אַחֲרָיו כְּבוֹדוֹ: 19 כִּי־ נַפְשׁוֹ בְּחַיָּיו יְבָרֵךְ וְיוֹדֻךָ כִּי־ תֵיטִיב לָךְ: 20 תָּבוֹא עַד־ דּוֹר אֲבוֹתָיו עַד־נֵצַח לֹא יִרְאוּ־אוֹר: 21 אָדָם בִּיקָר

<table>
<tr>
<td>

19   [1]He shall [a]go to the generation of his fathers;

    They will never see [b]the light.

20   [a]Man in *his* [1]pomp, yet without understanding,

    Is [b]like the [2]beasts that [3]perish.

</td>
<td>

וְלֹא יָבִין נִמְשַׁל כַּבְּהֵמוֹת נִדְמוּ׃

</td>
</tr>
</table>

References

Psalm 49:1
[a]Ps 78:1; Is 1:2; Mic 1:2
[b]Ps 33:8

Psalm 49:2
[a]Ps 62:9

Psalm 49:3
[a]Ps 37:30
[b]Ps 119:130

Psalm 49:4
[1]Lit *open up*
[a]Ps 78:2
[b]2 Kin 3:15
[c]Num 12:8

Psalm 49:5
[1]Lit *supplanters*
[a]Ps 23:4; 27:1

Psalm 49:6
[a]Job 31:24; Ps 52:7; Prov 11:28; Mark 10:24

Psalm 49:7
[a]Matt 25:8, 9
[b]Job 36:18, 19

Psalm 49:8
[1]Lit *their*
[a]Matt 16:26

Psalm 49:9
[1]Or *see corruption* or *the pit*
[a]Ps 22:29
[b]Ps 16:10; 89:48

Psalm 49:10

[a]Eccl 2:16
[b]Ps 92:6; 94:8
[c]Ps 39:6; Eccl 2:18, 21; Luke 12:20

Psalm 49:11

[1]Some versions read *graves are their houses*
[a]Ps 64:6
[b]Ps 10:6
[c]Gen 4:17; Deut 3:14

Psalm 49:12

[1]Lit *honor*
[2]Or *animals*
[3]Lit *are destroyed*
[a]Ps 49:20

Psalm 49:13

[1]*Selah* may mean: *Pause, Crescendo* or *Musical interlude*
[a]Jer 17:11
[b]Ps 49:18

Psalm 49:14

[1]I.e. the nether world
[2]Lit *Away from his habitation*
[a]Ps 9:17
[b]Dan 7:18; Mal 4:3; 1 Cor 6:2; Rev 2:26
[c]Job 24:19

Psalm 49:15

[1]Lit *hand*
[2]I.e. the nether world
[a]Ps 16:10; 56:13; Hos 13:14
[b]Gen 5:24; Ps 16:11; 73:24

Psalm 49:16

[1]Or *wealth*
[a]Ps 37:7

Psalm 49:17

[1]Or *wealth*

[a]Ps 17:14; 1 Tim 6:7

Psalm 49:18
[1]Lit *his soul*
[a]Deut 29:19; Ps 10:3, 6; Luke 12:19

Psalm 49:19
[1]Lit *You;* or *It*
[a]Gen 15:15
[b]Job 33:30; Ps 56:13

Psalm 49:20
[1]Lit *honor*
[2]Or *animals*
[3]Lit *are destroyed*
[a]Ps 49:12
[b]Eccl 3:19

Targum

Psa. 49:1 For praise; by the sons of Korah; a hymn. [2] Hear this declaration, all peoples; give ear, all dwellers on earth. [3] Even the sons of the first Adam, even the sons of Jacob together, righteous and sinner. [4] My mouth will speak wisdom, and the murmur of my heart is understanding. [5] I will incline my ear to a parable, I will begin to open my riddle with the lyre. [6] Why should I fear on the day of the visitation of evil, except that the guilt of my sin at my end will encompass me? [7] Woe to the sinners, who trust in their possessions, and who boast in the size of their riches. [8] A man will by no means redeem his brother, who was taken captive, by his riches; and he will not give to God his price of redemption. [9] And he gives his glorious redemption, and his evil will cease, and vengeance forever. [10] And he will live again for eternal life; he will not see the judgment of Gehenna. [11] For the wise will see the wicked, in Gehenna they will be judged; together fools and the stupid will perish, and they will leave their money to the righteous. [12] In their tomb they will abide forever, and they will not rise from their tents for all generations, because they have exalted themselves; and they have acquired an evil name upon the earth. [13] And a wicked man will not lodge in glory with the righteous; he is likened to a beast, he is worth nothing. [14] This their way has caused folly for them; and in their end with their mouth they will recount their offenses in the world to come. [15] Like sheep, they have assigned the righteous to death, and killed them; they have destroyed the righteous and those who serve the Torah, and the upright they have punished; because of this, their bodies will decay in Gehenna, because they extended their hand and wrecked the dwelling place of his Presence. [16] David said in the spirit of prophecy, "Truly, God will redeem my soul from the judgment of Gehenna, for he will teach me his Torah forever." [17] About Korah and his party he prophesied and said, "Do not fear, Moses, because Korah, the man of dispute, has become rich, because the glory of his house will increase." [18] For in his death he will keep nothing, his glory will not descend after him. [19] For the soul of Moses during his life will bless you; and the righteous will thank you, for you are good to those who worship in your presence. [20] The memory of the righteous will come to the generation of their fathers; but the wicked will not see light forever and ever. [21] The sinful man, when he is in honor, will have no insight; and when his honor is taken from him, he becomes like a beast and worth nothing. --

Spiritual Awareness

The spiritual rewrite for the verses is in bold.

Introduction

Korach's sons determined that their father's greed drove him to rebel against Moses. This is the concluding Psalm from them. In it are instructions about the relationship between material goods and spirituality. A person must enhance their spiritual being more than their riches. You cannot take riches with you. Your spiritual awareness and growth will always be with your soul.

Superscript

This is the superscript that is found in Psalms 40-48. The author calls upon the Sefirah Netzach for victory and strength.

To Him to grants victory, a psalm by the sons of Korach.

Verse one

The author calls for the reader to hear this message. Since Psalms were read to people, it is an alert to listen carefully.

Hear this carefully, for this message is for all people.

Verse two

גַּם־בְּנֵי אָדָם גַּם־בְּנֵי־אִישׁ (gam b'nai adam gam bnai ish) – means "also sons of men and sons of men." This phrase refers to people who derive some advantage through the fact they can trace their ancestry to men of distinction.

The message of this Psalm is for everyone, rich, poor, important, and not important.

People of distinction, rich and poor, come together.

Verse three

The reader is told that what is about to be read is the wisdom they should pay attention to.

My mouth is able to speak what is in accordance with wisdom, and the meditation of my heart what is seemly to understand.

Verse four

What is about to be said is not from the author's own wisdom. Instead, it is from Divine inspiration. The riddle is a "closed book" to the mind. It is opened when the solution to the riddle is had.

I will incline my ear to the parable; I shall solve my riddle upon the harp.

Verse five

The psalmist is concerned that he might not fulfill his true purpose in life.

Why should I fear when the iniquity of my enemies surrounds me in the days of evil?

Verses six, seven, and eight

The Psalmist addresses people who place their trust in material possession. One's trust should be their faith in the LORD.

As for people who put their trust in their wealth and glory in the multitude of riches,

And yet not one of them will redeem his brother with it, and thus does not give God an atonement,

For them, the redemption of their own soul is too costly, and it shall cease to be forever.

Verse nine

A person who depends on his/her wealth alone will find immortality challenging to purchase.

And yet he desires to live on in eternity. He does not wish to see decay.

Verses ten & eleven

Even though a rich person sees that people die and their wealth is distributed to others, they do not understand that wealth will not prevent them from dying. Over time their wealth will be distributed to the point that no one alive will remember them.

He sees wise men die, fools perish altogether, and leave their wealth to others.

And yet they think their houses are forever, their dwelling places from generation to generation, for they have proclaimed their names throughout the land.

Verse twelve

No person can outlast the night of death.

But a man with all his honor will not outlast the night if he is like the beasts that fall silent.

Verse thirteen

Wealthy people tend to hold onto their belief in their wealth even with life and death experiences.

This is the way of those who are foolish and of those after them who approve of their words. Meditate on this verse.

Verse fourteen

The grave was not to be their final destination. The LORD intends for all people to join Him in Heaven. It is a person's decision whether to follow the path of the LORD (spirituality) or the path of the Earth (materialism).

As sheep, they are appointed for Sheol. Death shall be their shepherd. The upright shall rule over them in the morning, and their form shall be for Sheol to consume so that they have no habitation.

Verse fifteen

But God will redeem my soul for the power of the grave by taking me to Himself. Meditate on this verse.

Verses sixteen and seventeen

Do not be upset when you see people with more incredible wealth and better fortune than you. Do not forfeit any of your true life values simply because your lot is humble compared to others. Remember that you cannot take wealth with you.

Therefore be not afraid when a person flaunts their wealth,

For when that person dies, he/she cannot take it with them.

Verse eighteen

A wicked person will praise himself and believe that others should pay tribute to him. People will praise you because you did well for yourself, honestly.

He blesses himself even during his lifetime, saying, "They will praise you because you have done well for yourself."

Verses nineteen and twenty

A person who flaunts wealth and does not share will not enter Heaven.

He shall go to the generation of his fathers; They will never see the light.

Man in his pomp, yet without understanding, is like the beasts that perish.

Complete Psalm Rewrite Emphasizing Spiritual Awareness

To Him to grants victory, a psalm by the sons of Korach.
Hear this carefully, for this message is for all people.

People of distinction, rich and poor, come together.

My mouth is able to speak what is in accordance with wisdom, and the meditation of my heart what is seemly to understand.

I will incline my ear to the parable; I shall solve my riddle upon the harp.

Why should I fear when the iniquity of my enemies surrounds me in the days of evil?

As for people who put their trust in their wealth and glory in the multitude of riches,

And yet not one of them will redeem his brother with it, and thus does not give God an atonement,

For them, the redemption of their own soul is too costly, and it shall cease to be forever.

And yet he desires to live on in eternity. He does not wish to see decay.

He sees wise men die, fools perish altogether, and leave their wealth to others.

And yet they think their houses are forever, their dwelling places from generation to generation, for they have proclaimed their names throughout the land.

But a man with all his honor will not outlast the night if he is like the beasts that fall silent.

This is the way of those who are foolish and of those after them who approve of their words. Meditate on this verse.

As sheep, they are appointed for Sheol. Death shall be their shepherd. The upright shall rule over them in the morning, and their form shall be for Sheol to consume so that they have no habitation.

But God will redeem my soul for the power of the grave by taking me to Himself. Meditate on this verse.

Therefore be not afraid when a person flaunts their wealth,

For when that person dies, he/she cannot take it with them.

He blesses himself even during his lifetime, saying, "They will praise you because you have done well for yourself."

He shall go to the generation of his fathers; They will never see the light.

Man in his pomp, yet without understanding, is like the beasts that perish.

Psalm 50

New American Standard 1995	Hebrew

Psa. 50:0   A Psalm of [†]Asaph.

Psa. 50:1   [a]The Mighty One, God, the LORD, has spoken,
  And summoned the earth [b]from the rising of the sun to its setting.
2   Out of Zion, [a]the perfection of beauty,
  God [b]has shone forth.
3   May our God [a]come and not keep silence;
  [b]Fire devours before Him,
  And it is very [c]tempestuous around Him.
4   He [a]summons the heavens above,
  And the earth, to judge His people:
5   "Gather My [a]godly ones to Me,
  Those who have made a [b]covenant with Me by [c]sacrifice."
6   And the [a]heavens declare His righteousness,
  For [b]God Himself is judge.
  [1]Selah.

Psa. 50:7   "[a]Hear, O My people, and I will speak;
  O Israel, I will testify [1]against you;
  I am God, [b]your God.
8   "I do [a]not reprove you for your sacrifices,
  And your burnt offerings are continually before Me.

מִזְמ֗וֹר לְאָ֫סָ֥ף אֵ֤ל **Psa. 50:1**
אֱלֹהִ֨ים ׀ יְהֹוָ֗ה דִּבֶּ֥ר וַיִּקְרָא־
אָ֑רֶץ מִמִּזְרַח־שֶׁ֝֗מֶשׁ עַד־
מְבֹאֽוֹ׃ 2 מִצִּיּ֥וֹן מִכְלַל־יֹ֝֗פִי
אֱלֹהִ֥ים הוֹפִֽיעַ׃ 3 יָ֤בֹא
אֱלֹהֵ֗ינוּ וְֽאַל־יֶ֫חֱרַ֥שׁ אֵשׁ־
לְפָנָ֥יו תֹּאכֵ֑ל וּ֝סְבִיבָ֗יו
נִשְׂעֲרָ֥ה מְאֹֽד׃ 4 יִקְרָ֣א אֶל־
הַשָּׁמַ֣יִם מֵעָ֑ל וְאֶל־הָ֝אָ֗רֶץ
לָדִ֥ין עַמּֽוֹ׃ 5 אִסְפוּ־לִ֥י
חֲסִידָ֑י כֹּרְתֵ֖י בְרִיתִ֣י עֲלֵי־
זָֽבַח׃ 6 וַיַּגִּ֣ידוּ שָׁמַ֣יִם צִדְק֑וֹ
כִּֽי־אֱלֹהִ֓ים ׀ שֹׁפֵ֖ט ה֣וּא
סֶֽלָה׃ 7 שִׁמְעָ֤ה עַמִּ֨י ׀
וַאֲדַבֵּ֗רָה יִ֭שְׂרָאֵל וְאָעִ֣ידָה
בָּ֑ךְ אֱלֹהִ֖ים אֱלֹהֶ֣יךָ אָנֹֽכִי׃ 8
לֹ֣א עַל־זְ֭בָחֶיךָ אוֹכִיחֶ֑ךָ
וְעוֹלֹתֶ֖יךָ לְנֶגְדִּ֣י תָמִֽיד׃ 9

9 "I shall take no [a]young bull out of your house

Nor male goats out of your folds.

10 "For [a]every beast of the forest is Mine,

The cattle on a thousand hills.

11 "I know every [a]bird of the mountains,

And everything that moves in the field is [1]Mine.

12 "If I were hungry I would not tell you,

For the [a]world is Mine, and [1]all it contains.

13 "Shall I eat the flesh of [1a]bulls

Or drink the blood of male goats?

14 "Offer to God [a]a sacrifice of thanksgiving

And [b]pay your vows to the Most High;

15 [a]Call upon Me in the day of trouble;

I shall [b]rescue you, and you will [c]honor Me."

Psa. 50:16 But to the wicked God says,

"What right have you to tell of My statutes

And to take [a]My covenant in your mouth?

17 "For you [a]hate discipline,

And you [b]cast My words behind you.

18 "When you see a thief, you [1a]are pleased with him,

And [2]you [b]associate with adulterers.

19 "You [1a]let your mouth loose in evil

And your [b]tongue frames deceit.

לֹא־אֶקַּח מִבֵּיתְךָ פָּר

10 : מִמִּכְלְאֹתֶיךָ עַתּוּדִים

כִּי־לִי כָל־חַיְתוֹ־יָעַר

11 : בְּהֵמוֹת בְּהַרְרֵי־אָלֶף

יָדַעְתִּי כָּל־עוֹף הָרִים וְזִיז

12 : שָׂדַי עִמָּדִי אִם־אֶרְעַב

לֹא־אֹמַר לָךְ כִּי־לִי תֵבֵל

13 : וּמְלֹאָהּ הַאוֹכַל בְּשַׂר

אַבִּירִים וְדַם עַתּוּדִים

14 : אֶשְׁתֶּה זְבַח לֵאלֹהִים

תּוֹדָה וְשַׁלֵּם לְעֶלְיוֹן נְדָרֶיךָ

15 : וּקְרָאֵנִי בְּיוֹם צָרָה

16 : אֲחַלֶּצְךָ וּתְכַבְּדֵנִי

וְלָרָשָׁע אָמַר אֱלֹהִים מַה־

לְּךָ לְסַפֵּר חֻקָּי וַתִּשָּׂא בְרִיתִי

17 : עֲלֵי־פִיךָ וְאַתָּה שָׂנֵאתָ

מוּסָר וַתַּשְׁלֵךְ דְּבָרַי

18 : אַחֲרֶיךָ אִם־רָאִיתָ גַנָּב

וַתִּרֶץ עִמּוֹ וְעִם מְנָאֲפִים

19 : חֶלְקֶךָ פִּיךָ שָׁלַחְתָּ

בְרָעָה וּלְשׁוֹנְךָ תַּצְמִיד

20 : מִרְמָה תֵּשֵׁב בְּאָחִיךָ

: תְדַבֵּר בְּבֶן־אִמְּךָ תִּתֶּן־דֹּפִי

²⁰ "You sit and ^aspeak against your brother;

You slander your own mother's son.

²¹ "These things you have done and ^aI kept silence;

You thought that I was just like you;

I will ^breprove you and state *the case* in order before your eyes.

Psa. 50:22 "Now consider this, you who ^aforget God,

Or I will ^btear *you* in pieces, and there will be none to deliver.

²³ "He who ^aoffers a sacrifice of thanksgiving honors Me;

And to him who ^{1b}orders *his* way *aright*

I shall ^cshow the salvation of God."

אֵ֤לֶּה עָשִׂ֨יתָ ׀ וְֽהֶחֱרַ֗שְׁתִּי דִּמִּ֗יתָ הֱ‍ֽיוֹת־אֶֽהְיֶ֥ה כָמ֑וֹךָ אוֹכִֽיחֲךָ֖ וְאֶֽעֶרְכָ֣ה לְעֵינֶֽיךָ׃ 21

בִּֽינוּ־נָ֣א זֹ֭את שֹׁכְחֵ֣י אֱל֑וֹהַּ פֶּן־אֶ֝טְרֹ֗ף וְאֵ֣ין מַצִּֽיל׃ 22

זֹבֵ֥חַ תּוֹדָ֗ה יְֽכַבְּדָ֫נְנִי וְשָׂ֥ם דֶּ֑רֶךְ אַ֝רְאֶ֗נּוּ בְּיֵ֣שַׁע אֱלֹהִֽים׃ 23

ReferencesPsalm 50:0
[1] 1 Chr 15:17; 2 Chr 29:30

Psalm 50:1
[a] Josh 22:22
[b] Ps 113:3

Psalm 50:2
[a] Ps 48:2; Lam 2:15
[b] Deut 33:2; Ps 80:1; 94:1

Psalm 50:3
[a] Ps 96:13
[b] Lev 10:2; Num 16:35; Ps 97:3; Dan 7:10
[c] Ps 18:12, 13

Psalm 50:4
[a] Deut 4:26; 31:28; 32:1; Is 1:2

Psalm 50:5
[a] Ps 30:4; 37:28; 52:9
[b] Ex 24:7; 2 Chr 6:11; Ps 25:10
[c] Ps 50:8

Psalm 50:6
[1] *Selah* may mean: *Pause, Crescendo* or *Musical interlude*
[a] Ps 89:5; 97:6
[b] Ps 75:7; 96:13

Psalm 50:7
[1] Or *to*
[a] Ps 49:1; 81:8
[b] Ex 20:2; Ps 48:14

Psalm 50:8
[a] Ps 40:6; 51:16; Is 1:11; Hos 6:6

Psalm 50:9
[a] Ps 69:31

Psalm 50:10
[a] Ps 104:24

Psalm 50:11
[1]Or *in My mind;* lit *with Me*
[a]Matt 6:26

Psalm 50:12
[1]Lit *its fullness*
[a]Ex 19:5; Deut 10:14; Ps 24:1; 1 Cor 10:26

Psalm 50:13
[1]Lit *strong ones*
[a]Ps 50:9

Psalm 50:14
[a]Ps 27:6; 69:30; 107:22; 116:17; Hos 14:2; Rom 12:1; Heb 13:15
[b]Num 30:2; Deut 23:21; Ps 22:25; 56:12; 61:8; 65:1; 76:11

Psalm 50:15
[a]Ps 91:15; 107:6, 13; Zech 13:9
[b]Ps 81:7
[c]Ps 22:23

Psalm 50:16
[a]Is 29:13

Psalm 50:17
[a]Prov 5:12; 12:1; Rom 2:21, 22
[b]1 Kin 14:9; Neh 9:26

Psalm 50:18
[1]Some ancient versions read *run together*
[2]Lit *your part is with*
[a]Rom 1:32
[b]1 Tim 5:22

Psalm 50:19
[1]Lit *send*
[a]Ps 10:7
[b]Ps 36:3; 52:2

Psalm 50:20
[a]Job 19:18; Matt 10:21

Psalm 50:21
[a]Eccl 8:11; Is 42:14; 57:11
[b]Ps 90:8

Psalm 50:22
[a]Job 8:13; Ps 9:17
[b]Ps 7:2

Psalm 50:23
[1]Lit *sets*
[a]Ps 50:14
[b]Ps 85:13
[c]Ps 91:16

Targum

Psa. 50:1 A hymn composed by Asaph. Mighty is God; the LORD spoke at the Creation a song; and he carved out the earth from the rising of the sun to its setting. **2** The perfection and the beginning of the eternal creation is from Zion; and from there its beauty is complete, God will be revealed. **3** The righteous will say on the great day of judgment, "Our God will come, and he will not neglect to vindicate his people"; fire will blaze before him, and around him a storm will rage mightily. **4** He will call to the angels of the height above, and to the righteous of the earth below, to extend judgment to his people. **5** Gather to me, my pious ones, who have made my covenant, and fulfilled my Torah, and have engaged in prayer, which is likened to a sacrifice. **6** And the angels of the height will recount his righteousness, for God is the judge forever. **7** Hear, O my people, and I will speak, O Israel; and I will testify to you; I am God, your God. **8** I am not rebuking you on account of your sacrifices that you did not offer before me in exile, for your holocausts that your fathers offered are in front of me always. **9** From the day that my sanctuary was laid waste, I have not accepted a bull from your hands, or rams from your flock. **10** For mine are all the animals of the forest, and I have prepared for the righteous in the Garden of Eden clean beasts and a wild bull who grazes every day on a thousand mountains. **11** Manifest before me are all the kinds of birds who fly in the air of heaven; and the rooster whose legs rest on the earth, while his head reaches to heaven, rejoicing before me. **12** If the time of the continual morning sacrifice should arrive, I would not tell you; for mine is the earth and its fullness. **13** From the day my sanctuary was laid waste, I have not accepted the flesh of the sacrifice of fatlings, and the priests have not sprinkled the blood of rams before me. **14** Subdue the evil impulse and it will be reckoned before the LORD as a sacrifice of thanksgiving; and pay to the Most High your vows. **15** And pray in my presence in the day of trouble; I will save you, for you will glorify me. **16** But to the wicked who has not repented, and prays in impiety, the LORD says, "Why do you recite my covenant, and swear by my name, and invoke my covenant with your mouth?" [17] But you hate the rebuke of the wise, and you have cast my words behind you. [18] If you saw a thief, you ran after him; and you have placed your portion with adulterers. [19] You have loosened your mouth to utter evil speech ; and your tongue adheres to speaking deceit. [20] You will sit with your brother, you will speak lies against your mother's son, you will cast aspersions. [21] These bad deeds you did and I waited for you to repent; you thought you would be at peace forever; you said in your heart, "I will be strong like you"; I will rebuke you in this world, and I will prepare the judgment of Gehenna before you in the world to come. [22] Now understand this, you wicked who have forgotten God, lest I break your might, with no one to save. [23] He who sacrifices the evil impulse, it will be reckoned to him like a sacrifice of thanksgiving, and he honors me; and whoever will remove the evil way, I will show him the redemption of the LORD.

Spiritual Awareness

The spiritual rewrite for the verses is in bold.

Introduction

This Psalm describes the intense desire of the LORD to reveal Himself to his beloved Israel. However, the LORD will not make His presence known to His children until they desire it. One has to demonstrate a sincere desire to draw near him. The Psalmist indicates an effective means of drawing close to the LORD. This is accomplished by studying the meaning of the Torah. It is not enough to simply read the Torah. One has to learn the many levels of understanding in each passage. Rabbi Chiam of Volozhin said that Torah study makes a person worthy of being the LORD's son.

Superscript and verse one

אֵל (el) – means "God." The common usage of this word is to emphasize God as the "mighty God." This word's connotation is that the Psalmist refers to the strength of the LORD, which enables life, breathing, growth, and our ability to know the LORD.

A psalm of Asaf. The mighty God of Israel has spoken and calls forth from the earth from sunrise to sunset.

Verse two

Mount Zion became the place where the Word of the LORD given to Israel at Mount Sinai would reside during King David's time. It is on the Temple mount in Jerusalem, on Mount Zion, where Solomon built the LORD's house on earth. Ancient Israelites believed that the LORD's perfection and beauty always shined from the mountain. Zion is considered sacred today and will always be sacred.

Out of Zion, the epitome of beauty, the LORD has already appeared.

Verse three

The LORD reveals Himself utilizing His word. Israel sensed the presence of the LORD for the first time at Mount Sinai when Moses came down from the mountain with the two tablets of the LORD's word. That feeling will come to the people if they study the Torah.

The LORD will return and will not be silent; a fire devours before Him, and it is exceedingly stormy around Him.

Verse four

The LORD appointed the heaven and earth to be guarantors and witnesses to Israel's fulfillment of their promise to the LORD. The Ten Commandments is a treaty between the LORD and Israel. The LORD says that He will protect Israel. In turn, Israel agreed to live by the LORD's commandments. Now the LORD calls upon heaven and earth to be His witnesses and to proclaim His judgment over His people.

He calls to the heavens and the earth to judge His people.

Verse five

אִסְפוּ (es'foo) – means "gather" and it is in possessive form. This word denotes a gathering into one spiritual unit. Judgment is against the entire nation, not individually. People believe they will be individually judged in the Modern and Post-Modern world. Since no one has returned from the dead to tell us the process, this point is hard to debate. However, in this Psalm, the Psalmist says that Israel will be judged as one large spiritual unit and not individually.

Gather as one spiritual unit My devoted persons who uphold My covenant as they perform the rite of sacrifice.

Verse six

And the heavens declare His righteousness, for God Himself is the judge. Meditate upon this verse.

Verse seven

The Psalmist tells us that the LORD has something to say to His people. This is a serious thing so pay attention. Above all things, the LORD expects His people to worship Him as the guide to one's deeds and as the ruler of one's destiny. "To testify against you "means telling the people what they are doing wrong."

Hear, O My people, I wish to speak; O Israel I wish to testify against you; I am God, your God.

Verses eight to twelve

The LORD reminds us that He is the ultimate owner of everything.

> **I do not reprove you for your sacrifices, and your burnt offerings are continually before Me.**
>
> **I shall take no young bull out of your house nor male goats out of your folds.**
>
> **For every beast of the forest is Mine, the cattle on a thousand hills.**
>
> **I know every bird of the mountains, and everything that moves in the field is Mine.**
>
> **If I were hungry I would not tell you, for the world is Mine, and all it contains.**

Verse thirteen

The LORD does not eat meat, nor does He drink blood. The LORD did command Israel to offer sacrifices of flesh and blood. The sacrifices were never to afford the LORD the sensual pleasure of devouring flesh and blood. The flesh symbolized the sacrifice of the strength of your muscles while working within the LORD's laws which brings His favor. The blood signifies the consecration of a person's spirit so that it may strive upwards to the high plane at which it will meet the LORD's favor.

The spiritual awareness of the sacrificial system was first an acknowledgment that the LORD is the creator of all things. It is through the Shekinah that the presence of the LORD is given to those who seek it. Without the Light of the LORD through the Shekinah and the Nukvah of Binah nothing would exist. Raising an animal that can be sacrificed to the LORD required time and resources. The work required to feed and care for the animal would be rewarded by the LORD because sacrificing the animal shows trust in the LORD and that one does not expect anything special from the LORD. It is a mitzvah to sacrifice something to the LORD without any expectations. The LORD does reward His people who make the sacrifice without strings attached nor expecting something in return.

Ancient people believed that one's spirit was in one's blood. Therefore, the blood sacrifice symbolizes giving one's spirit to live following the Torah. It was a reminder that one must place complete trust and faith in the LORD. By following the Torah, a person proves their covenant.

But do I eat the flesh of bulls or drink the blood of goats?

Verse fourteen

The Psalmist reminds us that it is important to acknowledge the gifts from the LORD daily.

Offer an acknowledgment to God and give your vows to the Most High.

Verse fifteen

Turn to the LORD in times of trouble. The covenant between the LORD and His people will renew with every offering.

Call upon Me in times of trouble, says the LORD; I will make you free, and you will honor me.

Verse sixteen

Wicked people are those who know the statutes of the LORD and have decided to ignore them. The LORD demands to know why some people think it is okay to do this.

To the wicked, God says, What right have you to violate my statutes and to speak about my covenant?

Verse seventeen

Every word in the Torah has explicit implications upon our desires and ambitions, speech and actions, and thus banishes sin from our midst.

For you hate discipline, and you cast my words behind you.

Verse eighteen

The LORD tells the people that some are not thieves or adulterers; however, they approve of them because they allow them to circumvent the law. Today this is equivalent to major US city District Attorneys not prosecuting criminals. In 2022 one can shoplift $950 of merchandise in California and not go to jail. The leaders of California may not be criminals. Still, since they allow criminal activities to go unpunished, the LORD says they are guilty.

When you see a thief, you are pleased with him and associate with adulterers.

Verses nineteen & twenty

These verses are directed at the wicked people of the world. The LORD accuses them of expounding the Torah, but they use deceit and slander when committing their crimes.

You have let loose your mouth for evil, and your tongue frames deceit.

If you sit, you speak against your brother; you slander your own mother's son.

Verse twenty-one

The LORD said that since lawless acts had gone unpunished, the people must have thought that the LORD agreed. The LORD wants lawless people punished for their actions. It is wrong for devout people to allow the wicked to continue in their ways.

These things you have done and I have kept silent; therefore, you thought that, in fact, I was like yourself. Consequently, I reprove you and set it before your eyes.

Verse twenty-two

The LORD offers the wicked an opportunity to return to Him.

Now understand this, you who have forgotten God, lest I could tear in pieces and there is none to deliver.

Verse twenty-three

Salvation is found in the LORD.

He who offers acknowledgment honors Me in truth, and to him who bases his way of life thereon, I shall show the salvation of God.

Verse twenty-three

Complete Psalm Rewrite Emphasizing Spiritual Awareness

A psalm of Asaf. The mighty God of Israel has spoken and calls forth from the earth from sunrise to sunset.

Out of Zion, the epitome of beauty, the LORD has already appeared.

The LORD will return and will not be silent; a fire devours before Him, and it is exceedingly stormy around Him.

He calls to the heavens and the earth to judge His people.

Gather as one spiritual unit My devoted persons who uphold My covenant as they perform the rite of sacrifice.

And the heavens declare His righteousness, for God Himself is the judge. Meditate upon this verse.

Hear, O My people, I wish to speak; O Israel I wish to testify against you; I am God, your God.

I do not reprove you for your sacrifices, and your burnt offerings are continually before Me.

I shall take no young bull out of your house nor male goats out of your folds.

For every beast of the forest is Mine, the cattle on a thousand hills.

I know every bird of the mountains, and everything that moves in the field is Mine.

If I were hungry I would not tell you, for the world is Mine, and all it contains.

But do I eat the flesh of bulls or drink the blood of goats?

Offer an acknowledgment to God and give your vows to the Most High.

Call upon Me in times of trouble, says the LORD; I will make you free, and you will honor me.

To the wicked, God says, What right have you to violate my statutes and to speak about my covenant?

For you hate discipline, and you cast my words behind you.

When you see a thief, you are pleased with him and associate with adulterers.

You have let loose your mouth for evil, and your tongue frames deceit.

If you sit, you speak against your brother; you slander your own mother's son.

These things you have done and I have kept silent; therefore, you thought that, in fact, I was like yourself. Consequently, I reprove you and set it before your eyes.

Now understand this, you who have forgotten God, lest I could tear in pieces and there is none to deliver.

He who offers acknowledgment honors Me in truth, and to him who bases his way of life thereon, I shall show the salvation of God.

Appendix

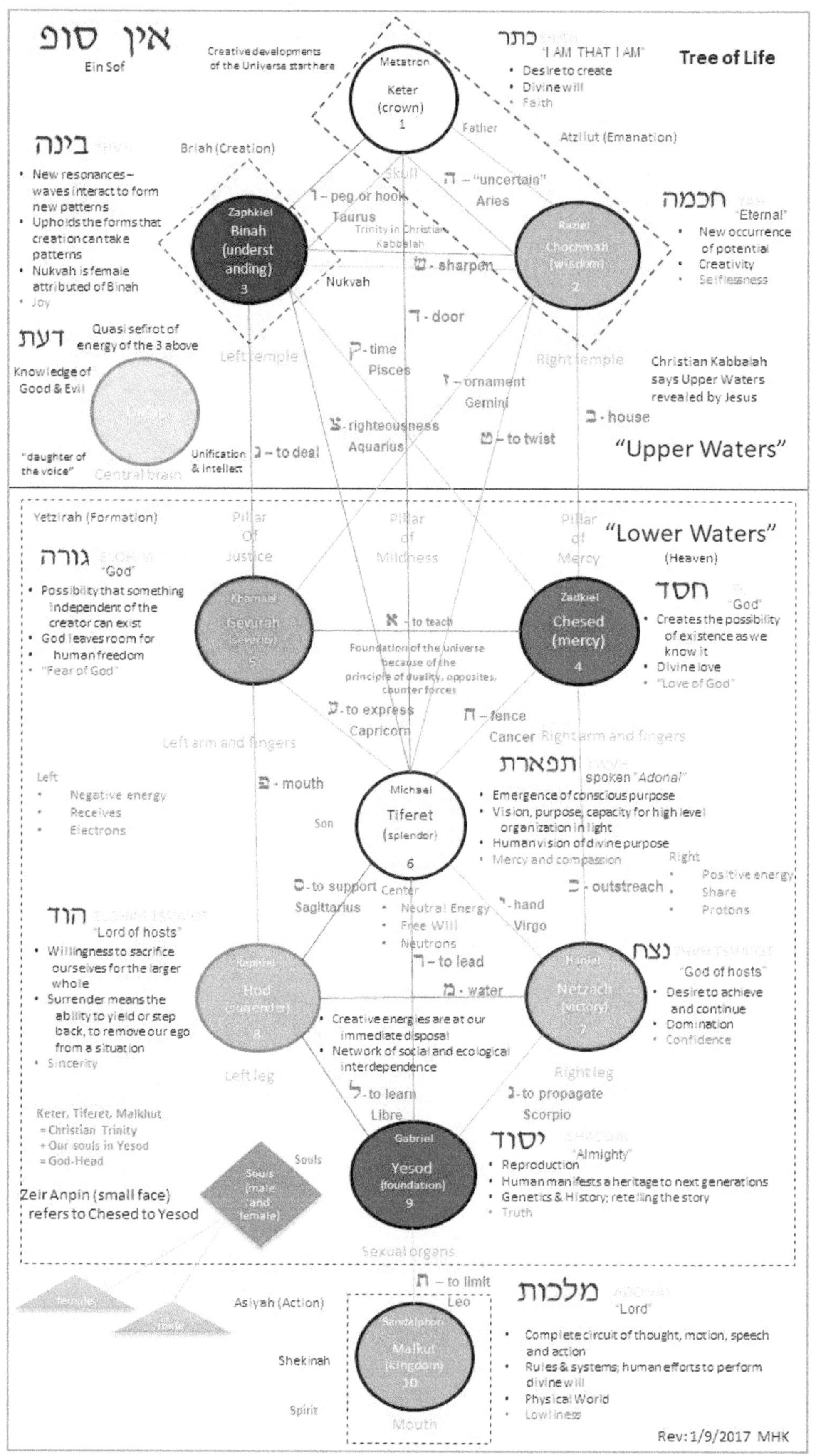
אין סוף
Ein Sof
Creative developments of the Universe start here
כתר
"I AM THAT I AM"
• Desire to create
• Divine will
• Faith
Tree of Life
Metatron
Keter (crown)
1
Father
Atzilut (Emanation)
בינה
• New resonances – waves interact to form new patterns
• Upholds the forms that creation can take patterns
• Nukvah is female attributed of Binah
• Joy
Briah (Creation)
Zaphkiel
Binah (understanding)
3
ו – peg or hook
Taurus
Trinity in Christian Kabbalah
Nukvah
ה – "uncertain"
Aries
ש - sharpen
חכמה
"Eternal"
• New occurrence of potential
• Creativity
• Selflessness
Raziel
Chochmah (wisdom)
2
דעת
Quasi sefirot of energy of the 3 above
Knowledge of Good & Evil
"daughter of the voice"
Da'at
Central brain
Left temple
ד - door
ק - time
Pisces
ז – ornament
Gemini
צ - righteousness
Aquarius
נ – to deal
Unification & intellect
Right temple
ב - house
ל - to twist
Christian Kabbalah says Upper Waters revealed by Jesus
"Upper Waters"
Yetzirah (Formation)
Pillar Of Justice
Pillar of Mildness
Pillar of Mercy
"Lower Waters"
(Heaven)
גבורה
"God"
• Possibility that something independent of the creator can exist
• God leaves room for human freedom
• "Fear of God"
Khamael
Gevurah (severity)
5
Left arm and fingers
א – to teach
Foundation of the universe because of the principle of duality, opposites, counter forces
ע - to express
Capricorn
Zadkiel
Chesed (mercy)
4
ח – fence
Cancer
Right arm and fingers
חסד
"God"
• Creates the possibility of existence as we know it
• Divine love
• "Love of God"
תפארת
spoken "Adonai"
• Emergence of conscious purpose
• Vision, purpose, capacity for high level organization in light
• Human vision of divine purpose
• Mercy and compassion
Michael
Tiferet (splendor)
6
Son
פ - mouth
Left
• Negative energy
• Receives
• Electrons
Right
• Positive energy
• Share
• Protons
כ - to support
Sagittarius
Center
• Neutral Energy
• Free Will
• Neutrons
ר – to lead
מ - water
כ - outreach
י - hand
Virgo
הוד
"Lord of hosts"
• Willingness to sacrifice ourselves for the larger whole
• Surrender means the ability to yield or step back, to remove our ego from a situation
• Sincerity
Raphael
Hod (surrender)
8
Left leg
ל - to learn
Libra
נצח
"God of hosts"
• Desire to achieve and continue
• Domination
• Confidence
Haniel
Netzach (victory)
7
Right leg
ב - to propagate
Scorpio
Keter, Tiferet, Malkhut
= Christian Trinity
+ Our souls in Yesod
= God-Head
Zeir Anpin (small face) refers to Chesed to Yesod
Souls (male and female)
Souls
Creative energies are at our immediate disposal
Network of social and ecological interdependence
Gabriel
Yesod (foundation)
9
יסוד
"Almighty"
• Reproduction
• Human manifests a heritage to next generations
• Genetics & History; retelling the story
• Truth
Sexual organs
ט – to limit
Leo
Asiyah (Action)
Shekinah
Spirit
Sandalphon
Malkut (kingdom)
10
Mouth
מלכות
"Lord"
• Complete circuit of thought, motion, speech and action
• Rules & systems; human efforts to perform divine will
• Physical World
• Lowliness
Rev: 1/9/2017 MHK

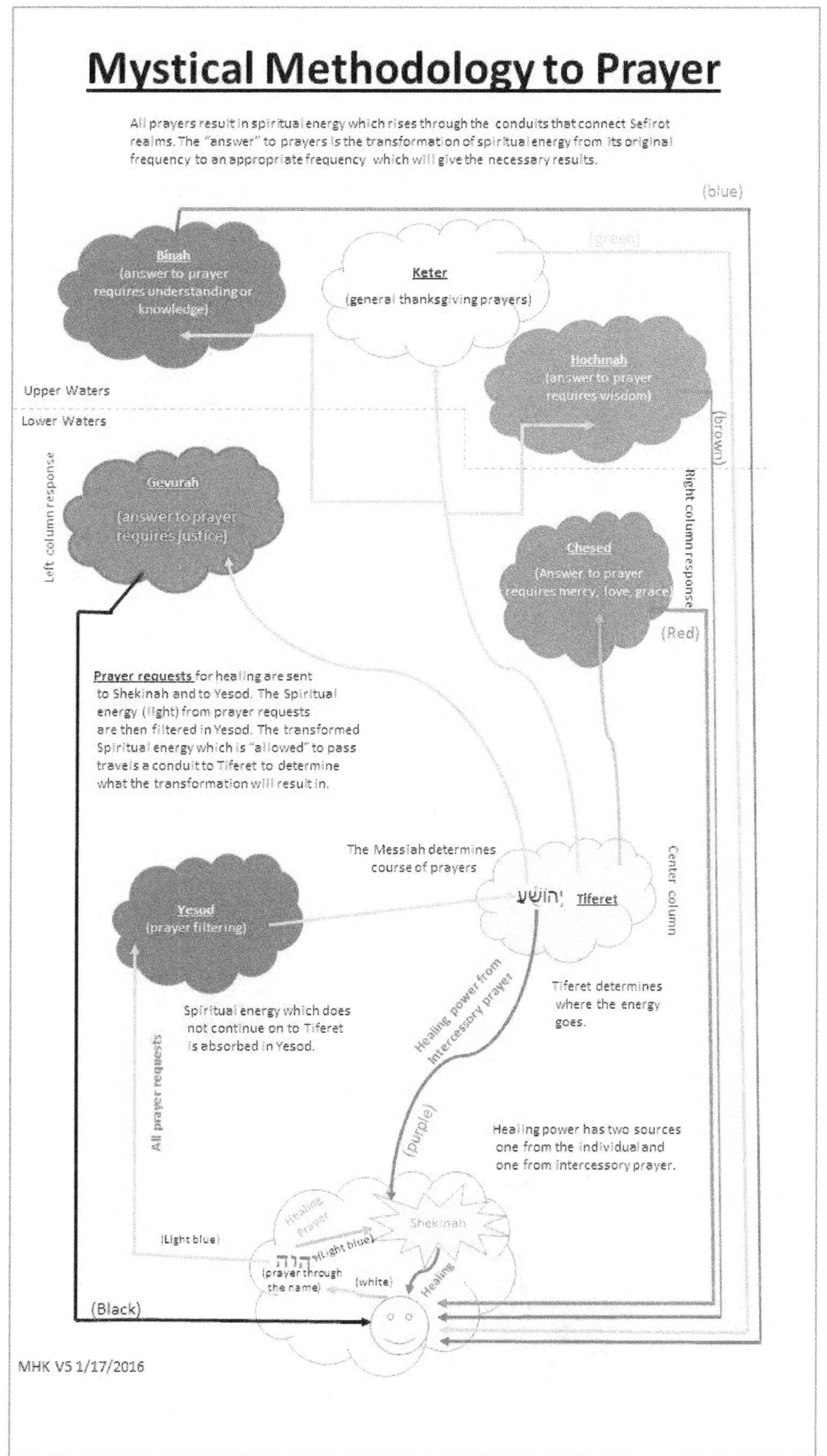

Mystical Methodology to Prayer
All prayers result in spiritual energy which rises through the conduits that connect Sefirot realms. The "answer" to prayers is the transformation of spiritual energy from its original frequency to an appropriate frequency which will give the necessary results.
(blue)
(green)
(brown)
(Red)
Binah
(answer to prayer requires understanding or knowledge)
Keter
(general thanksgiving prayers)
Hochmah
(answer to prayer requires wisdom)
Upper Waters
Lower Waters
Left column response
Gevurah
(answer to prayer requires justice)
Chesed
(Answer to prayer requires mercy, love, grace)
Right column response
Prayer requests for healing are sent to Shekinah and to Yesod. The Spiritual energy (light) from prayer requests are then filtered in Yesod. The transformed Spiritual energy which is "allowed" to pass travels a conduit to Tiferet to determine what the transformation will result in.
The Messiah determines course of prayers
יְהוֹשֻׁעַ   Tiferet
Center column
Yesod
(prayer filtering)
Tiferet determines where the energy goes.
Healing power from intercessory prayer
Spiritual energy which does not continue on to Tiferet is absorbed in Yesod.
All prayer requests
Healing power has two sources one from the individual and one from intercessory prayer.
(purple)
Healing Prayer
(Light blue)
(light blue)
Shekinah
יהוה
(prayer through the name)
(white)
Healing
(Black)
MHK V5 1/17/2016

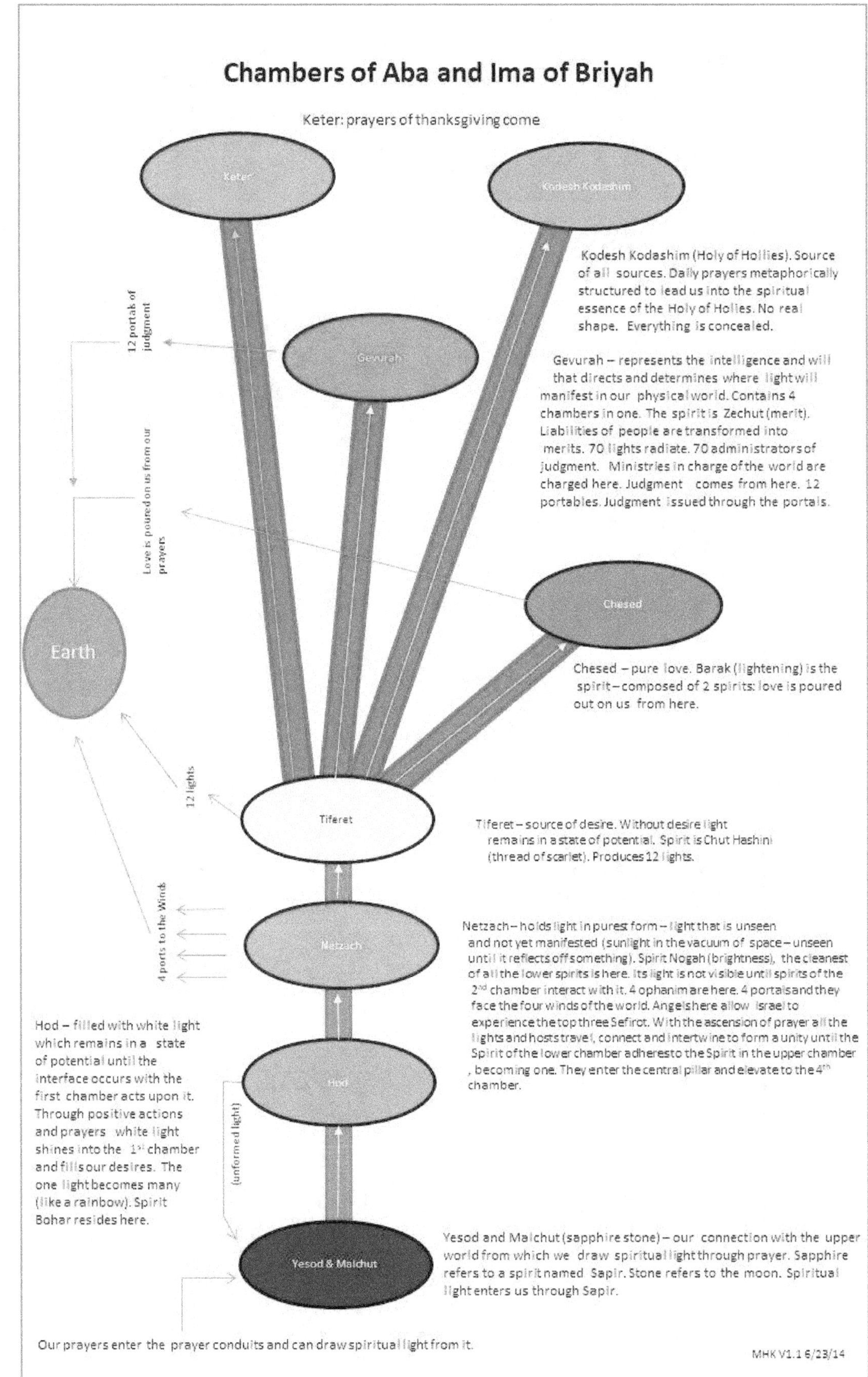

Chambers of Aba and Ima of Briyah

Keter: prayers of thanksgiving come

Keter

Kodesh Kodashim

Kodesh Kodashim (Holy of Hollies). Source of all sources. Daily prayers metaphorically structured to lead us into the spiritual essence of the Holy of Hollies. No real shape. Everything is concealed.

12 portals of judgment

Gevurah

Gevurah – represents the intelligence and will that directs and determines where light will manifest in our physical world. Contains 4 chambers in one. The spirit is Zechut (merit). Liabilities of people are transformed into merits. 70 lights radiate. 70 administrators of judgment. Ministries in charge of the world are charged here. Judgment comes from here. 12 portables. Judgment issued through the portals.

Love is poured on us from our prayers

Earth

Chesed

Chesed – pure love. Barak (lightening) is the spirit – composed of 2 spirits: love is poured out on us from here.

12 lights

Tiferet

Tiferet – source of desire. Without desire light remains in a state of potential. Spirit is Chut Hashini (thread of scarlet). Produces 12 lights.

4 ports to the Winds

Netzach

Netzach – holds light in purest form – light that is unseen and not yet manifested (sunlight in the vacuum of space – unseen until it reflects off something). Spirit Nogah (brightness), the cleanest of all the lower spirits is here. Its light is not visible until spirits of the 2nd chamber interact with it. 4 ophanim are here. 4 portals and they face the four winds of the world. Angels here allow Israel to experience the top three Sefirot. With the ascension of prayer all the lights and hosts travel, connect and intertwine to form a unity until the Spirit of the lower chamber adheres to the Spirit in the upper chamber, becoming one. They enter the central pillar and elevate to the 4th chamber.

Hod – filled with white light which remains in a state of potential until the interface occurs with the first chamber acts upon it. Through positive actions and prayers white light shines into the 1st chamber and fills our desires. The one light becomes many (like a rainbow). Spirit Bohar resides here.

Hod

(unformed light)

Yesod & Malchut

Yesod and Malchut (sapphire stone) – our connection with the upper world from which we draw spiritual light through prayer. Sapphire refers to a spirit named Sapir. Stone refers to the moon. Spiritual light enters us through Sapir.

Our prayers enter the prayer conduits and can draw spiritual light from it.

MHK V1.1 6/23/14

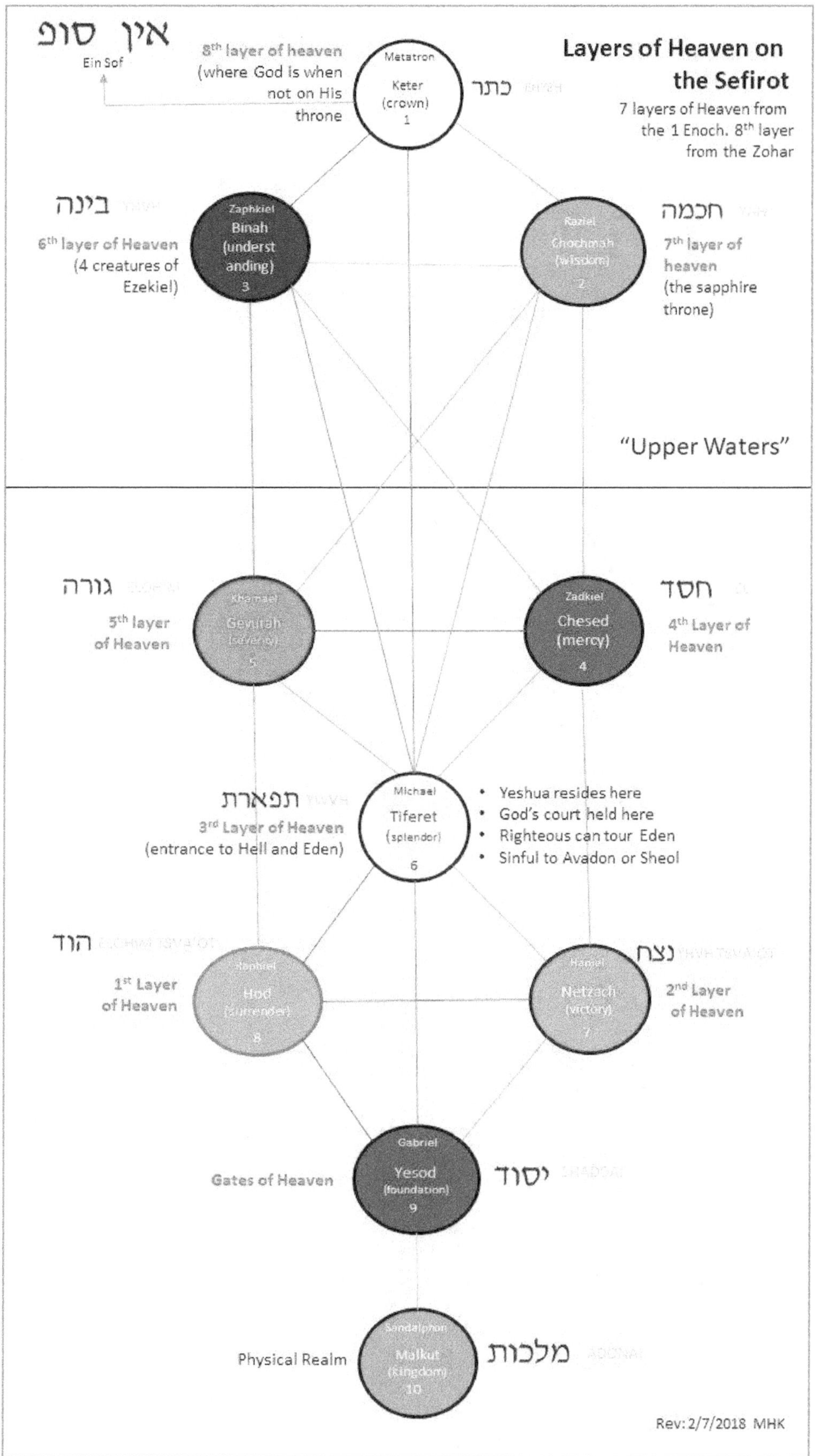
אין סוף
Ein Sof
8th layer of heaven (where God is when not on His throne)
Metatron
Keter (crown)
1
כתר
Layers of Heaven on the Sefirot
7 layers of Heaven from the 1 Enoch. 8th layer from the Zohar
בינה
6th layer of Heaven (4 creatures of Ezekiel)
Zaphkiel
Binah (understanding)
3
Raziel
Chochmah (wisdom)
2
חכמה
7th layer of heaven (the sapphire throne)
"Upper Waters"
גורה
5th layer of Heaven
Khamael
Gevurah (severity)
5
Zadkiel
Chesed (mercy)
4
חסד
4th Layer of Heaven
תפארת
3rd Layer of Heaven (entrance to Hell and Eden)
Michael
Tiferet (splendor)
6
Yeshua resides here
God's court held here
Righteous can tour Eden
Sinful to Avadon or Sheol
הוד
1st Layer of Heaven
Raphiel
Hod (surrender)
8
Haniel
Netzach (victory)
7
נצח
2nd Layer of Heaven
Gates of Heaven
Gabriel
Yesod (foundation)
9
יסוד
Physical Realm
Sandalphon
Malkut (kingdom)
10
מלכות
Rev: 2/7/2018 MHK